LAUGH AGAIN

Publications by Charles R. Swindoll

Books:

Come Before Winter
Compassion: Showing We Care in a Careless World
Dropping Your Guard
Encourage Me
For Those Who Hurt
The Grace Awakening
Growing Deep in the Christian Life
Growing Strong in the Seasons of Life
Hand Me Another Brick
Improving Your Serve
Killing Giants, Pulling Thorns
Leadership: Influence That Inspires
Living Above the Level of Mediocrity
Living Beyond the Daily Grind, Books 1 and 2
Living on the Ragged Edge
Make Up Your Mind
The Quest for Character
Recovery: When Healing Takes Time
Rise and Shine
Sanctity of Life
Simple Faith
Standing Out
Starting Over
Strengthening Your Grip
Stress Fractures
Strike the Original Match
The Strong Family
Three Steps Forward, Two Steps Back
Victory: A Winning Game Plan for Life
You and Your Child

Minibooks:

Abraham: A Model of Pioneer Faith
David: A Model of Pioneer Courage
Esther: A Model of Pioneer Independence
Moses: A Model of Pioneer Vision
Nehemiah: A Model of Pioneer Determination

Booklets:

Anger
Attitudes
Commitment
Dealing with Defiance
Demonism
Destiny
Divorce
Eternal Security
Fun Is Contagious
God's Will
Hope
Impossibilities
Integrity
Leisure
The Lonely Whine of the Top Dog
Moral Purity
Our Mediator
Peace . . . in Spite of Panic
Prayer
Sensuality
Singleness
Stress
Tongues
When Your Comfort Zone Gets the Squeeze
Woman

LAUGH AGAIN

CHARLES R. SWINDOLL

WORD PUBLISHING
Dallas·London·Vancouver·Melbourne

LAUGH AGAIN

Unless otherwise indicated, Scripture quotations used in this book are from the New American Standard Bible (NASB) © 1960, 1962, 1963, 1968, 1971, 1972, 1973, 1975, 1977 by The Lockman Foundation. Used by permission.

Other Scripture quotations are from the following sources:

The Holy Bible, New International Version (NIV). Copyright © 1973, 1978, 1984 International Bible Society. Used by permission of Zonder-van Bible Publishers.

The New Testament in Modern English (PHILLIPS) by J. B. Phillips, published by The Macmillan Company, © 1958, 1960, 1972 by J. B. Phillips.

The Good News Bible, Today's English Version (TEV)—Old Testament: Copyright © American Bible Society 1976; New Testament: Copyright © American Bible Society 1966, 1971, 1976.

The Living Bible (TLB), copyright 1971 by Tyndale House Publishers, Wheaton, Ill. Used by permission.

Library of Congress Cataloging-in-Publication Data

Swindoll, Charles R.
    Laugh again / Charles R. Swindoll.
        p.   cm.
    ISBN 0–8499–0957–0
    1. Joy—Religious aspects—Christianity.   2. Laughter—Religious
aspects—Christianity.   I. Title.
    BV4647.J68S95 1992
    248.4—dc20   92–17825
                                                              CIP

Printed in the United States of America

2 3 4 5 9   MP   9 8 7 6 5 4

This book is affectionately dedicated to
Al and Margaret Sanders
and
Jon and Peggy Campbell
with gratitude for their unselfish devotion
to the radio ministry of
Insight for Living.
It was the Sanderses' vision that launched the broadcasts and
the Campbells' commitment that sustained it during its infancy.
Because of their tireless involvement in and appreciation for the
ministry, I find myself encouraged and invigorated.
And because of their spirit of outrageous joy,
our times together are often punctuated
with fun and laughter.

Contents

Acknowledgments

The closest a man can come to understanding childbirth is by writing a book. Passing a kidney stone ranks right up there. I've had four of those, but that's another story.

The process of this particular bookbirth has been unusually delightful and relatively free of pain. Maybe after my many literary "kids," I'm getting the hang of it.

Those who have served as midwives are among the best in the business. Byron Williamson, Kip Jordan, Ernie Owen, and David Moberg of Word Publishing not only rejoiced to know I was "expecting," but they also helped name the baby and provided a colorful jacket for it to wear. In fact the whole atmosphere they brought to the delivery center was so pleasant, I found myself forgetting that it was supposed to be a difficult process.

Once again I want to express my gratitude to Helen Peters, who cleaned the baby up after it was born. Thanks also to Judith Markham and Ed Curtis, who again gave me wise editorial counsel and helpful ideas that would keep this newborn healthy and strong. As all my immediate family members either came by to visit or phoned to see how I was feeling as I was moving closer to the delivery date, my spirits were lifted. And, as always, Cynthia was especially encouraging, knowing how concerned I was that this be a happy baby and free of needless complications. Her supportive presence proved crucial.

Finally, I want to declare my gratitude to my Great Physician who allowed me to meet with Him regularly without a scheduled appointment, provided excellent checkups, demonstrated compassionate care, and assisted me in the birth with gentleness and joy. I knew that everything was going to be all right because immediately after it was born, something most unusual happened. Unlike all the others I have had, when this one finally came, it laughed.

I am grateful for you too. As you hold it close and enjoy its company, may its happy disposition bring you hours of delight. All I ask is that when it smiles at you, smile back. If you do, you will soon discover a bond forming between the two of you that will lighten your load and help you relax. It is a funny thing about babies—the way they curl up in our arms and become a part of our lives the longer we spend time with them. Who knows? At some unguarded moment when you two are all alone and no one else is watching, you might even break down and laugh again. Feel free. As a proud parent, I can't think of anything that would please me more.

Introduction

This is a book about joy.

It's about relaxing more, releasing the tension, and refusing to let circumstances dominate our attitudes.

It's about looking at life from a perspective other than today's traffic report or the evening news.

It's about giving the child within us permission to look at life and laugh again.

Can you remember when life was joyful? I certainly can. Without any knowledge of the Dow index or the drop in the gross national product or the accelerating crime rate in twenty-five of America's largest cities or the decreasing health-care benefits in our country's major companies, I was happy as a clam. I neither expected much nor needed much. Life was meant to be enjoyed, not endured, and therefore every day I found something—anything—to laugh about.

Through my childlike eyes people were funny. (When did they stop being funny?) When school was out and those lazy, hazy months of summer were mine to enjoy, there was usually enough water somewhere to swim in or a basketball to dribble and shoot hoops with or old roller skates to make a sidewalk scooter from or a crazy joke to laugh at. (When did everything get so serious?)

Our family of five had no wealth whatsoever. My dad was a machinist, often holding down more than one job to make ends meet. My mom stayed home and did all the stuff moms do at home with three strong-willed, very normal kids. Since there was a war raging on both sides of our nation, we had a truckload of reasons not to laugh . . . but I never got that message back then. I was a child and I did what children did. We made music in our family, another relaxing pastime. Some of it was pretty scary music, but we laughed that off too. And why not? I mean, it wasn't like we were rehearsing for Carnegie Hall or hoping to get a scholarship to the Juilliard School of Music. We were just having fun . . . and music was the creative avenue we chose to enjoy. Boy, did we ever! (Why have families stopped making music together?)

While flying back from Germany in the fall of 1990, I met a delightful man with an infectious laugh. It was fascinating talking with him, and as we talked, I learned that he speaks all around the world and brings joy to thousands, from prisoners to presidents. As you can imagine, he had one great story after another, most of them true and each one absolutely hilarious. Our multiple-hour flight passed all too quickly.

One of my favorites makes me smile every time I recall it. This incident actually happened to the woman who passed the story on to my fellow passenger.

Grandmother and granddaughter, a very precocious ten-year-old, were spending the evening together when the little girl suddenly looked up and asked, "How old are you, Grandma?"

The woman was a bit startled at the question, but knowing her granddaughter's quick little mind, she wasn't completely shocked.

"Well, honey, when you're my age you don't share your age with anybody."

"Aw, go ahead, Grandma . . . you can trust me."

"No, dear, I never tell anyone my age."

Grandmother got busy fixing supper and then she suddenly realized the little darling had been absent for about twenty minutes—much too long! She checked around upstairs in her bedroom and found that her granddaughter had dumped the contents of her grandmother's purse on top of her bed and was sitting in the midst of the mess, holding her grandmother's driver's license.

When their eyes met, the child announced: "Grandma, you're seventy-six."

"Why, yes, I am. How did you know that?"

"I found the date of your birthday here on your driver's license and subtracted that year from this year . . . so you're seventy-six!"

"That's right, sweetheart. Your grandmother is seventy-six."

The little girl continued staring at the driver's license and added, "You also made an F in sex, Grandma."[1]

Sometime between that age of childhood innocence and right now, life has become a grim marathon of frowns—a major downer for far too many adults. I suppose some would justify the change by saying, "When you become an adult, you need to be responsible." I couldn't agree more.

I had that drilled into my cranium. (Remember, my middle name starts with an R!) Furthermore, the same ones would say, "Being responsible includes living in a world of reality, and not everything in the real world is funny. Some things are extremely difficult." Again, you're speaking my language. Having been engaged in real-world responsibilities for well over thirty of my adult years, I am painfully aware that this old earth is not a giant bowl of cherries. They continue, "So then, since adulthood is a synonym for responsibility, and since reality certainly includes difficulties, we have no business laughing and enjoying life." It's at that point of the logic I balk. I simply do not accept the notion that responsible people in touch with the real world must wear a perpetually serious countenance and adopt a grim-reaper mind-set.

My question is this: When did a healthy, well-exercised sense of humor get sacrificed on the altar of adulthood? Who says becoming a responsible adult means a long face and an all-serious attitude toward life?

My vocation is among the most serious of all professions. As a minister of the gospel and as the senior pastor of a church, the concerns I deal with are eternal in dimension. A week doesn't pass without my hearing of or dealing with life in the raw. Marriages are breaking, homes are splitting, people are hurting, jobs are dissolving, addictions of every description are rampant. Needs are enormous, endless, and heartrending.

The most natural thing for me to do would be to allow all of that to rob me of my joy and to change me from a person who has always found humor in life—as well as laughed loudly and often—into a stoic, frowning clergyman. No thanks.

Matter of fact, that was my number-one fear many years ago. Thinking that I must look somber and be ultraserious twenty-four hours a day resulted in my resisting a call into the ministry for several years. Most of the men of the cloth I had seen looked like they held down a night job at the local mortuary. I distinctly remember wrestling with the Lord over all this before He pinned me to the mat and whispered a promise in my ear that forced me to surrender: "You can faithfully serve Me, but you can still be yourself. Being My servant doesn't require you to stop laughing." That did it. That one statement won me over. I finally decided I could be one of God's spokesmen and still enjoy life.

Not too many years ago when I started the radio program, "Insight for Living," I flashed back to that original call, and I decided to be myself, no matter what. Whether the broadcasts succeeded or fizzled, I wasn't about to come across as some superpious religious fanatic, intense about everything. When things struck me funny, I would laugh.

One of the listeners wrote in and commented: "I appreciate your program. The teaching has helped a lot . . . but I have one major request: Don't stop laughing! You can stop teaching and you can make whatever other changes you wish on your broadcasts, but *don't stop laughing!*" And then she added: "Yours is the only laughter that comes into our home."

Her ten concluding words have been ringing in my ears for years. What a sad commentary on our times! In many homes—dare I say most?—laughter has left. Joy that was once a vital ingredient in family life has departed, leaving hearts that seldom sing, lips that rarely smile, eyes that no longer dance, and faces that say no. Tragically, this is true in Christian homes as well as non-Christian . . . maybe more so.

It is my firm conviction that a change is urgently needed—which is precisely why I have taken up my pen to write again. A couple of years ago I warned of grace killers and urged my readers to be courageous as they joined the ranks of the grace-awakening movement. Many have done so. Later, I became concerned about all the complicated busywork many were adding to the life of faith, so I exposed the faith crushers as I encouraged folks to cultivate a simple-faith lifestyle. Many have done that as well. Maybe you are one of them. Now, within the last few months, I have felt an urgent need to take on the joy stealers who have been growing in number, especially since recessionary times have hit. Bad news has become the only news.

Tough times are upon us, no question. The issues we all face are both serious and real. But are they so intense, so all-important, so serious and all-consuming that every expression of joy should be eclipsed? Sorry, I can't buy that.

This book will tell you why. Hopefully, as a result of traveling through its pages with me, you will gain a new perspective on how to view these harsh days. Best of all, many of your childlike qualities will emerge and soften the blows of your intensity. Your attitude will change. You will find yourself changing. How will you know? There is one telltale sign. You'll begin to laugh again.

Chuck Swindoll
Fullerton, California

Where there is no belief in the soul, there is very little drama. . . . Either one is serious about salvation or one is not. And it is well to realize that the maximum amount of seriousness admits the maximum amount of comedy. Only if we are secure in our beliefs can we see the comical side of the universe.

Flannery O'Connor

1

Your Smile Increases Your Face Value

I KNOW OF NO GREATER NEED today than the need for joy. Unexplainable, contagious joy. Outrageous joy.

When that kind of joy comes aboard our ship of life, it brings good things with it—like enthusiasm for life, determination to hang in there, and a strong desire to be of encouragement to others. Such qualities make our voyage bearable when we hit the open seas and encounter high waves of hardship that tend to demoralize and paralyze. There is nothing better than a joyful attitude when we face the challenges life throws at us.

Someone once asked Mother Teresa what the job description was for anyone who might wish to work alongside her in the grimy streets and narrow alleys of Calcutta. Without hesitation she mentioned only two things: the desire to work hard and a joyful attitude. It has been my observation that both of those qualities are rare. But the second is much rarer than the first. Diligence may be difficult to find, but compared to an attitude of genuine joy, hard work is commonplace.

Unfortunately, our country seems to have lost its spirit of fun and laughter. Recently, a Brazilian student studying at a nearby university told me that what amazes him the most about Americans is their lack of laughter. I found myself unable to refute his criticism.

Just look around. Bad news, long faces, and heavy hearts are everywhere—even in houses of worship (especially in houses of worship!). Much of today's popular music, which many consider a voice for the nation's conscience, promotes misery, sorrow, and despair. If sex and violence are not the pulsating themes of a new film, some expression of unhappiness is. Newspapers thrive on tragedies and calamities, lost jobs and horrible accidents. The same can be said of televised newscasts. Even the weather reports give their primary attention to storms, droughts, and blizzards. Tomorrow is usually "partly cloudy with a 20 percent chance of rain," never "mostly clear with an 80 percent chance of sunshine." If you do find laughter on the tube, either it is a recorded laugh track on some stupid sitcom or a stand-up comedian telling filthy jokes.

This long-faced, heavy-hearted attitude has now invaded the ranks of Christianity. Visit most congregations today and search for signs of happiness and sounds of laughter and you often come away disappointed. Joy, "the gigantic secret of the Christian,"[1] is conspicuous by its absence. I find that *inexcusable*. The one place on earth where life's burdens should be lighter, where faces should reflect genuine enthusiasm, and where attitudes should be uplifting and positive is the place this is least likely to be true.

When I was a teenager, the most popular business advertisements in magazines read: SEND ME A MAN WHO READS. As much as I value reading and applaud the resourcefulness of those who pore over the pages of good books, I think today's slogan should be: SEND ME ONE WHOSE ATTITUDE IS POSITIVE, WHOSE HEART IS FULL OF CHEER, WHOSE FACE SHOUTS YES!

Some critics would be quick to point out that our times do not lend themselves to such an easygoing philosophy. They would ask, "Under these circumstances how could I be anything but grim?" To which I reply, "What are you doing *under* the circumstances?" Correct me if I'm wrong, but isn't the Christian life to be lived *above* the circumstances?

A good sense of humor enlivens our discernment and guards us from taking everything that comes down the pike too seriously. By remaining lighthearted, by refusing to allow our intensity to gain the mastery of our minds, we remain much more objective. Ogden Nash believed this so strongly that he claimed that if the German people had had a sense of humor, they would never have let Adolf Hitler deceive them. Instead, the first time they saw some fellow goose-stepping and raising a stiff arm to shout, "Heil Hitler," they'd have keeled over in sidesplitting laughter.[2]

People who live above their circumstances usually possess a well-developed sense of humor, because in the final analysis that's what gets them through. I met such a person at a conference in Chicago several years ago. We shared a few laughs following a session at which I had spoken. Later she wrote to thank me for adding a little joy to an otherwise ultraserious conference. (Why are most Christian conferences ultraserious?) Her note was a delightfully creative expression of one who had learned to balance the dark side of life with the bright glow of laughter. Among other things she wrote:

> Humor has done a lot to help me in my spiritual life. How could I have reared twelve children, starting at age 32, and not have had a sense of humor?
>
> After your talk last night I was enjoying some relaxed moments with friends I met here. I told them I got married at age 31. I didn't worry about getting married; I left my future in God's hands. But I must tell you, every night I hung a pair of men's pants on my bed and knelt down to pray this prayer:
>
> > Father in heaven, hear my prayer,
> >   And grant it if you can;
> > I've hung a pair of trousers here,
> >   Please fill them with a man.

The following Sunday I read that humorous letter to our congregation, and they enjoyed it immensely. I happened to notice the different reactions of a father and his teenaged son. The dad laughed out loud, but the son seemed preoccupied. On that particular Sunday the mother of this family had stayed home with their sick daughter. Obviously neither father nor son mentioned the story, because a couple of weeks later I received a note from the mother:

> Dear Chuck:
>
> I am wondering if I should be worried about something. It has to do with our son. For the last two weeks I have noticed that before our son turns the light out and goes to sleep at night, he hangs a woman's bikini over the foot of his bed. . . . Should I be concerned about this?

I assured her there was nothing to worry about. And I am pleased to announce that the young man recently married, so maybe the swimsuit idea works.

Perhaps you find yourself among those in the if-only group. You say you would laugh *if only* you had more money . . . *if only* you had more talent or were more beautiful . . . *if only* you could find a more fulfilling job? I challenge those excuses. Just as more money never made anyone generous and more talent never made anyone grateful, more of *anything* never made anyone joyful.

The happiest people are rarely the richest, or the most beautiful, or even the most talented. Happy people do not depend on excitement and 'fun' supplied by externals. They enjoy the fundamental, often very simple, things of life. They waste no time thinking other pastures are greener; they do not yearn for yesterday or tomorrow. They savor the moment, glad to be alive, enjoying their work, their families, the good things around them. They are adaptable; they can bend with the wind, adjust to the changes in their times, enjoy the contests of life, and feel themselves in harmony with the world. Their eyes are turned outward; they are aware, compassionate. They have the capacity to love.[3]

Without exception, people who consistently laugh do so *in spite of,* seldom *because of* anything. They pursue fun rather than wait for it to knock on their door in the middle of the day. Such infectiously joyful believers have no trouble convincing people around them that Christianity is real and that Christ can transform a life. Joy is the flag that flies above the castle of their hearts, announcing that the King is in residence.

MEET A MAN WHO SMILED IN SPITE OF . . .

There once lived a man who became a Christian as an adult and left the security and popularity of his former career as an official religious leader to follow Christ. The persecution that became his companion throughout the remaining years of his life was just the beginning of his woes. Misunderstood, misrepresented, and maligned though he was, he pressed on joyfully. On top of all that, he suffered from a physical ailment so severe he called it a "thorn in my flesh"—possibly an intense form of migraine that revisited him on a regular basis.

By now you know I am referring to Saul of Tarsus, later called Paul. Though not one to dwell on his own difficulties or ailments, the apostle did take the time to record a partial list of them in his second letter to his friends in Corinth. Compared to his first-century contemporaries, he was—

. . . in far more imprisonments, beaten times without number, often in danger of death. Five times I received from the Jews thirty-nine lashes. Three times I was beaten with rods, once I was stoned, three times I was shipwrecked, a night and a day I have spent in the deep. I have been on frequent journeys, in dangers from rivers, dangers from robbers, dangers from my countrymen, dangers from the Gentiles, dangers in the city, dangers in the wilderness, dangers on the sea, dangers among false brethren; I have been in labor and hardship, through many sleepless nights, in hunger and thirst, often without food, in cold and exposure. Apart from such external things, there is the daily pressure upon me of concern for all the churches.

2 Corinthians 11:23–28

Although that was enough hardship for several people, Paul's journey got even more rugged as time passed. Finally he was arrested and placed under the constant guard of Roman soldiers to whom he was chained for two years. While he was allowed to remain "in his own rented quarters" (Acts 28:30), the restrictions must have been irksome to a man who had grown accustomed to traveling and to the freedom of setting his own agenda. Yet not once do we read of his losing patience and throwing a fit. On the contrary, he saw his circumstances as an opportunity to make Christ known as he made the best of his situation.

READ A LETTER WITH A SURPRISING THEME

Interestingly, Paul wrote several letters during those years of house arrest, one of which was addressed to a group of Christians living in Philippi. It is an amazing letter, made even more remarkable by its recurring theme—joy. Think of it! Written by a man who had known excruciating hardship and pain, living in a restricted setting chained to a Roman soldier, the letter to the Philippians resounds with joy! Attitudes of joy and contentment are woven through the tapestry of these 104 verses like threads of silver. Rather than wallowing in self-pity or calling on his friends to help him escape or at least find relief from these restrictions, Paul sent a surprisingly lighthearted message. And on top of all that, time and again he urges the Philippians (and his readers) to be people of joy.

Let me show you how that same theme resurfaces in each of the four chapters.

• When Paul prayed for the Philippians, he smiled!

I thank my God in all my remembrance of you, always offering prayer *with joy* in my every prayer for you all.

Philippians 1:3–4

23

- When he compared staying on earth to leaving and going to be with Jesus, he was joyful.

> For to me, to live is Christ, and to die is gain. But if I am to live on in the flesh, this will mean fruitful labor for me; and I do not know which to choose. But I am hard-pressed from both directions, having the desire to depart and be with Christ, for that is very much better; yet to remain on in the flesh is more necessary for your sake. And convinced of this, I know that I shall remain and continue with you all for your progress and *joy in the faith*.

Philippians 1:21–25

- When he encouraged them to work together in harmony, his own joy intensified as he envisioned that happening.

> If therefore there is any encouragement in Christ, if there is any consolation of love, if there is any fellowship of the Spirit, if any affection and compassion, *make my joy complete* by being of the same mind, maintaining the same love, united in spirit, intent on one purpose.

Philippians 2:1–2

- When he mentioned sending a friend to them, he urged them to receive the man joyfully.

> But I thought it necessary to send to you Epaphroditus, my brother and fellow worker and fellow soldier, who is also your messenger and minister to my need; because he was longing for you all and was distressed because you had heard that he was sick. For indeed he was sick to the point of death, but God had mercy on him, and not on him only but also on me, lest I should have sorrow upon sorrow. Therefore I have sent him all the more eagerly in order that when you see him again you may *rejoice* and I may be less concerned about you. Therefore *receive him in the Lord with all joy*, and hold men like him in high regard.

Philippians 2:25–29

- When he communicated the "core" of what he wanted them to hear from him, he was full of joy.

> Finally, my brethren, *rejoice in the Lord*. To write the same things again is no trouble to me, and it is a safeguard for you.

Philippians 3:1

- When he was drawing his letter to a close, he returned to the same message of joy:

> *Rejoice in the Lord* always; again I will say, rejoice!
>
> *Philippians 4:4*

- Finally, when Paul called to mind their concern for his welfare, the joy about which he writes is (in my opinion) one of the most upbeat passages found in Scripture.

> But I *rejoiced* in the Lord greatly, that now at last you have revived your concern for me; indeed, you were concerned before, but you lacked opportunity. Not that I speak from want; for I have learned to be content in whatever circumstances I am. I know how to get along with humble means, and I also know how to live in prosperity; in any and every circumstance I have learned the secret of being filled and going hungry, both of having abundance and suffering need. I can do all things through Him who strengthens me. Nevertheless, you have done well to share with me in my affliction. And you yourselves also know, Philippians, that at the first preaching of the gospel, after I departed from Macedonia, no church shared with me in the matter of giving and receiving but you alone; for even in Thessalonica you sent a gift more than once for my needs. Not that I seek the gift itself, but I seek for the profit which increases to your account. But I have received everything in full, and have an abundance; I am amply supplied, having received from Epaphroditus what you have sent, a fragrant aroma, an acceptable sacrifice, well-pleasing to God. And my God shall supply all your needs according to His riches in glory in Christ Jesus.
>
> *Philippians 4:10–19*

NEEDED: A JOY TRANSFUSION

I strongly suspect that after the Philippians received this delightful little letter from Paul, their joy increased to an all-time high. They had received a joy transfusion from someone they dearly loved, which must have been all the more appreciated as they remembered Paul's circumstance. If he, in that irritating, confining situation, could be so positive, so full of encouragement, so affirming, certainly those living in freedom could be joyful.

Life's joy stealers are many, and you will need to get rid of them if you hope to attain the kind of happiness described by Paul's pen. If you don't, all attempts to receive (or give) a joy transfusion will be blocked. One of the ringleaders you'll need to do battle with sooner rather than later is that sneaky thief who slides into your thoughts and reminds you of something from the past that demoralizes you (even though it is over and done with and fully forgiven) or conjures up fears regarding something in the future (even though that frightening something may never happen). Joyful people stay riveted to the present—the here and now, not the then and never.

Helen Mallicoat made a real contribution to your life and mine when she wrote:

> I was regretting the past
> And fearing the future . . .
> Suddenly my Lord was speaking:
> "MY NAME IS I AM." He paused.
> I waited. He continued,
>
> "WHEN YOU LIVE IN THE PAST,
>   WITH ITS MISTAKES AND REGRETS,
>   IT IS HARD. I AM NOT THERE.
>   MY NAME IS NOT *I WAS.*
>
> "WHEN YOU LIVE IN THE FUTURE,
>   WITH ITS PROBLEMS AND FEARS,
>   IT IS HARD. I AM NOT THERE.
>   MY NAME IS NOT *I WILL BE.*
>
> "WHEN YOU LIVE IN THIS MOMENT,
>   IT IS NOT HARD.
>   I AM HERE.
>   MY NAME IS *I AM.*"[4]

IF GOD IS GOD . . . THEN LAUGHTER FITS LIFE

As I attempt to probe the mind of Paul, trying to find some common denominator, some secret clue to his joy, I have to conclude that it was his confidence in God. To Paul, God was in full control of everything. Everything! If hardship came, God permitted it. If pain dogged his steps, it was only because God allowed it. If he was under arrest, God still remained the sovereign director of his life. If there seemed to be no way out, God knew he was pressed. If things broke open and all pressure was relieved, God was responsible.

My point? God is no distant deity but a constant reality, a very present help whenever needs occur. So? So live like it. And laugh like it! Paul did. While he lived, he drained every drop of joy out of every day that passed. How do I know? This little letter to the Philippians says so—as we shall see in the following chapters.

- In the first chapter of Philippians we learn *there is laughter in living*—whether or not we get what we want, in spite of difficult circumstances, and even when there are conflicts.

- In the second chapter we learn *there is laughter in serving*. It starts with the right attitude (humility), it is maintained through right theology (God is God), and it is encouraged by right models and mentors (friends like Timothy and Epaphroditus).

- In the third chapter, we learn *there is laughter in sharing* as Paul shares three happy things: his testimony, his goal of living, and his reason for encouragement.

- Finally, in the fourth chapter we learn *there is laughter in resting*. These have to be some of the finest lines ever written on the principle of personal contentment.

What a treasure house of joy! Frankly, I'm excited—and I know you will be too. Before we are very far along, you will begin to realize that joy is a choice. You will discover that each person must choose joy if he or she hopes to laugh again.

Jesus gave us His truth so that His joy might be in us. And when that happens, our joy is full (John 15:11). The tragedy is that so few choose to live joyfully.

Will you? If you will, I can make you a promise: laughter and enthusiasm will follow.

I came across a story in one of Tim Hansel's books that points this out in an unforgettable way. It's the true account of an eighty-two-year-old man who had served as a pastor for over fifty of those years. In his later years he struggled with skin cancer. It was so bad that he had already had fifteen skin operations. Tim writes:

Besides suffering from the pain, he was so embarrassed about how the cancer had scarred his appearance, that he wouldn't go out. Then one day he was given *You Gotta Keep Dancin'* in which I tell of my long struggle with the chronic, intense pain from a near-fatal climbing accident. In that book, I told of the day when I realized that the pain would be with me forever. At that moment, I made a pivotal decision. I knew that it was up to me to choose how I responded to it. So I chose joy. . . .

After reading awhile, the elderly pastor said he put the book down, thinking, "He's crazy. I can't choose joy."

So he gave up on the idea. Then later he read in John 15:11 that joy is a gift. Jesus says, "I want to give you my joy so that your joy may be complete."

A *gift!* he thought. He didn't know what to do, so he got down on his knees. Then he didn't know what to say, so he said, "Well, then, Lord, *give it to me.*"

And suddenly, as he described it, this incredible hunk of joy came from heaven and landed on him.

"I was overwhelmed," he wrote. "It was like the joy talked about in Peter, a 'joy unspeakable and full of glory.' I didn't know what to say, so I said, 'Turn it on, Lord, turn it on!'" And before he knew it, he was dancing around the house. He felt so joyful that he actually felt born again—again. And this astonishing change happened at the age of 82.

He just had to get out. So much joy couldn't stay cooped up. So he went out to the local fastfood restaurant and got a burger. A lady saw how happy he was, and asked, "How are you doing?"

He said, "Oh, I'm wonderful!"

"Is it your birthday?" she asked.

"No, honey, it's better than that!"

"Your anniversary?"

"Better than that!"

"Well, what is it?" she asked excitedly.

"It's the joy of Jesus. Do you know what I'm talking about?"

The lady shrugged and answered, "No, I have to work on Sundays."[5]

Every time I read Tim's story, I shake my head. What a ridiculous response! But not unusual. Basically there are two kinds of people: people who choose joy and people who don't. People who choose joy pay no attention to what day of the week it is . . . or how old they are . . . or what level of pain they are in. They have deliberately decided to laugh again because they have chosen joy. People who do not choose joy miss the relief laughter can bring. And because they do not, they cannot. And because they can't, they won't.

Which one are you?

2

Set Your Sails for Joy

*T*HIS YEAR I TURN FIFTY-EIGHT. Thought I might as well let the whole world know.

When you're my age you discover that your closest friends are the most unmerciful in the cards they send you. Last year, at fifty-seven, it was one insult after another! Like, "Confound your enemies. Amaze your friends. Blow out *all* your candles!"

Another said on the front: "Wish I could be there to help you light your birthday candles . . . ," and on the inside, "but I'll be watching the glow in the sky and thinking of you."

That one was from Helen Peters, my longtime executive assistant who has typed every book I have written . . . someone you would expect to be compassionate and caring toward a guy my age, right? Wrong.

Several more mentioned the cake and candles, one warning me of two dangers: the candles would melt the frosting in fifteen seconds, so blow them out as fast as possible. Once that happens, however, the smoke alarm is likely to go off.

Garfield, the ornery cat, appears on the front of another. He is lying down (naturally) and thinking (with one eye open), "You can tell you're getting older when you wake up with that awful 'morning after' feeling . . . and you didn't do anything the night before!"

When you are this age—matter of fact, when you are *any* age—a sense of humor is essential. I once heard a great talk from a veteran missionary who spoke on "What I Would Pack in My Suitcase If I Were to Return to the Mission Field." The first item he named? A sense of humor. A friend of mine who once served the Lord for several years on foreign soil has a similar saying: "You need two things if you want to be happy in God's work overseas: a good sense of humor and no sense of smell!"

I have discovered that a joyful countenance has nothing to do with one's age or one's occupation (or lack of it) or one's geography or education or marital status or good looks or circumstances. As I wrote earlier—and will continue to write throughout this book—joy is a choice. It is a matter of attitude that stems from one's confidence in God—that He is at work, that He is in full control, that He is in the midst of whatever has happened, is happening, and will happen. Either we fix our minds on that and determine to laugh again, or we wail and whine our way through life, complaining that we never got a fair shake. We are the ones who consciously determine which way we shall go. To paraphrase the poet:

> One ship sails east
> One ship sails west
> Regardless of how the winds blow.
> It is the set of the sail
> And not the gale
> That determines the way we go.[1]

Laughing one's way through life depends on nothing external. Regardless of how severely the winds of adversity may blow, we set our sails toward joy.

I witnessed a beautiful example of this several months ago. Being one of the members of Dallas Seminary's Board of Regents, I have the privilege of interviewing new faculty members. At that particular time we were meeting with four of their newest faculty members, one of whom was a woman. Not just any woman, but the *first* woman ever invited to join the distinguished ranks of the faculty of Dallas Theological Seminary.

Lucy Mabery is her name, and several of us on the board flashed back as she told us of her pilgrimage. We have known Lucy for years.

This delightful, intelligent woman was rearing a family, teaching Bible classes, and busily engaged in a dozen other involvements while happily married to Dr. Trevor Mabery, a successful physician who was at the zenith of his career. Then her whole world caved in.

Trevor was flying back to Dallas with three other men from a Montana retreat, where they had been with Dr. James Dobson, discussing and praying about the Focus on the Family ministry. Their plane crashed, and all four of the men perished in the accident.

Shock waves stunned the city of Dallas. All four men were public figures and highly respected. Their widows were left to pick up the pieces of their own lives and begin again.

Lucy chose to do it with joy. Without a moment's warning, her beloved Trevor was gone. Grief, one of the most vicious of all the joy stealers, tore into the Mabery family like a tornado at full force. But, determined not to be bound by the cords of perpetual grief, Lucy remained positive, keen thinking, and joyful.

As we interviewed Lucy that day, her eyes sparkled with a delightful sense of humor, and her smile was contagious.

We asked what it was like to be the first woman serving on the faculty. With a smile she answered, "I have had great warmth and reception from the faculty members. Now the student body," she added, "is another story." We asked how she handled the more conservative male students who didn't agree with her being in that position. She said, "Oh, I take them to lunch and we talk about things. They soften a bit." After a brief pause, she added, "It's been a joyous experience. As a matter of fact, I was given an award from the student body recently for being the best-dressed woman faculty member!"

How can a person in Lucy's situation recover, pick up the pieces, and go on? How does anyone press on beyond grief? How do you still laugh at life? How do you put your arms around your children as a new single parent and help them laugh at the future? It comes from deep within—because people like Lucy Mabery set their sails for joy regardless of how the wind blows.

Lucy has a quiet confidence. Not in the long life of a husband and not in the fact that external circumstances always will be placid, peaceful, and easy, but in God, who is at work, who is in control, and who is causing all things to result in His greater glory. When you and I focus on that, we too discover we can laugh again, even after the horror of an airplane crash and the loss of our life's partner. Everything, I repeat, is determined by how we set our sails.

A SMALL BUT POWERFUL LETTER

All of this leads us quite naturally into the magnificent though brief letter to the Philippians. Although it contains only 104 verses, this delightful piece of inspired mail brings a smile to the faces of all who read it. Why? Because of the one who wrote it! In customary first-century manner he signs his name at the beginning rather than at the end—Paul. What memories must have swirled in the minds of his friends in Philippi when they read that name. Ten years ago this man had been in their midst, founding their church. Ten years ago he had been tossed into jail, though he had committed no crime. Ten years ago they had seen God work in pulling together a small group of young Christians in this unique Roman colony. And now, a decade later, they read the name again. It must have thrilled them just to see that name resurface. Like art-loving Italians . . . thrilled by the works of Michelangelo, like sixteenth-century German believers who were inspired by a spokesman named Martin Luther, like nineteenth-century black Americans who grasped at every word from Abraham Lincoln, like twentieth-century patriotic Britons who needed a Winston Churchill to help them hold fast, the people of the church at Philippi respected and needed Paul. He was their founder and friend. He was their teacher, their able and much-admired leader.

But Paul doesn't simply sign his name to this letter. He also mentions Timothy, a name that means "he who honors God." Timothy is mentioned alongside Paul, not because he wrote the letter, but because he was known to the Philippians, loved by them, and would soon visit them. The first-century dynamic duo: Paul and Timothy! I would imagine the Philippians could not wait to hear what Paul had to say.

From Servants to Saints

Instead of introducing themselves as "Paul and Timothy, hotshot celebrities," or "Paul and Timothy, superleaders," or "Paul and Timothy, men whom you must respect," the apostle writes, "Paul and Timothy, *servants*." Don't you like that? That's why Paul was great. He didn't act like a prima donna who had to be worshiped, or a fragile hero who had to be treated with kid gloves. He saw himself as a servant.

The Greek term translated *servant* means many things: One bound to another . . . by the bands of constraining love . . . one in such close relationship to another that only death could break the bond . . . one whose will is swallowed up in the sweet will of God . . . one who serves another [Christ] . . . with reckless abandon, not regarding his or her own interests.[2] Those words defined Paul and Timothy.

Interestingly, this is a letter from servants to saints. "Paul and Timothy . . . to all the saints in Christ Jesus in Philippi, including overseers and deacons"(1:1). Today we might say, "to pastors and deacons" or to "elders and deacons."

Saints is a very interesting term. If you've traveled in Europe, you have seen a lot of stone saints in and around huge cathedrals. If you worship in a liturgical church, you have seen them in icons—plaster or marble statues representing people whose lives have become famous in the long and colorful history of the church.

In my reading I came across a fascinating article entitled "On Making Saints." It was not referring to the manufacture of oversize statues, but of the process whereby people today are "sainted."

"Pope John Paul II has been sainting more men and women than all of his predecessors in the 20th century taken together,"[3] writes the author, who goes on to explain the lengthy process behind naming someone as an official saint. You have to know who to contact and what steps to take. I should also add, you need a pretty good slug of money to saint people.

But the saints Paul was writing to were not those kinds of saints. The saints in Philippi were ordinary people. They were everyday, normal folks like you and me. We seldom put common names in that light, but we could! Saint Chuck. Saint Frank. Saint Shirley. Saint Cynthia. Saint Sylvester. Saint Margaret. Saint Bob. Saint You. That's right—you!

The Greek term translated *saint* is from a word that means "set apart and consecrated for the purpose of God's service." Isn't that a great idea? That's why you are a saint. When you were born into God's family by faith in the Lord Jesus Christ, you got that title. You were set apart for God's special purpose. Consecration is at the core of the word.

"Paul and Timothy, servants of the living Christ, to all those set apart for the purpose of serving God, who live in the city of Philippi"; that's the idea.

Both Grace and Peace

And what does Paul offer these saints? "Grace and peace." (I love that.) Grace is something that comes to us which we don't deserve. Peace is something that happens within us which is not in any way affected by our external circumstances. With grace from above and peace within, who wouldn't have cause for rejoicing?

In its earliest form the word *peace* meant "to bind together" and came to include the whole idea of being bound so closely together with something or someone that a harmony resulted. The right woman who is joined in harmony with the right man in marriage begins a "peaceful" companionship. One friend who is joined in heart and soul to another friend sustains a "peaceful" relationship where harmony exists. When there is such grace-and-peace harmony, choosing joy flows naturally. And that certainly explains why Paul remained joyful. He had every reason not to. But he deliberately chose joy. Paul set his sails on the very things he offered his friends in Philippi, grace and peace.

JOYFUL THANKSGIVING

What was it about those folks in Philippi that brought Paul so much joy?

First, *he had happy memories of the people.*

> I thank my God in all my remembrance of you, always offering prayer with joy in my every prayer for you all, in view of your participation in the gospel from the first day until now.
>
> *Philippians 1:3–5*

His memory of them made him smile. Meaning what? What were Paul's happy memories? He had no regrets, he nursed no ill feelings, he struggled through no unresolved conflicts. When he looked back over a full decade and thought of the Philippians, he laughed!

I wonder how many pastors can say that about former churches they have served? Could you say that about former friends you have had? Or places where you have worked? Are yours happy memories? Unfortunately, the memory of certain people makes us churn. When we call them to mind, they bring sad or disappointing mental images. Paul knew no such memories from his days in Philippi. Amazingly, he could not remember one whom he would accuse or feel ill toward, not even those who threw him in prison or those who stood in a courtroom and made accusations against him. He entertained only good memories of Philippi. Positive memories make life so much lighter.

Another reason he was joyful? *He had firm confidence in God.*

> For I am confident of this very thing, that He who began a good work in you will perfect it until the day of Christ Jesus. For it is only right for me to feel this way about you all, because I have you in my heart, since

both in my imprisonment and in the defense and confirmation of the gospel, you all are partakers of grace with me.

Philippians 1:6–7

Paul's confidence in God was a settled fact. He knew that God was at work and in control. He was confident that God was bringing about whatever was happening for His greater glory. When we possess that kind of confidence, we have a solid platform built within us—a solid platform upon which joy can rest.

Look back at the words *began* and *perfect*. They represent opposite ends or, if you will, the *bookends* of life. The One who *started* (began) a good work in your life will *complete* (perfect) it.

> The work You have in me begun
> Will by Your grace be fully done.[4]

That's what gives us confidence. That's what helps us laugh again.

Focus on the word *perfect*. I doubt that we have imagined the true meaning of it. Travel back in your mind to the cross where Christ was crucified. See the Savior lifted up, paying for the sins of the world. Listen to His words. There were seven sayings that Christ uttered from the cross, commonly called the seven last words of Christ. One of them our Lord cried out was a single word, *Tetelestai!* Translated, it means, "It is finished!" *Telos* is the root Greek term, the same root of the word translated *perfect*. Paul was saying, "He who began a good work in you when you were converted ten years ago, Philippians, will bring it to completion. It will be finished! Jesus will see to it. And that gives me joy."

You want a fresh burst of encouragement? You may have a good friend who is not walking as close to the Lord as he or she once was. Here is fresh hope. Rest in the confidence that God has neither lost interest nor lost control. The Lord has not folded His arms and looked the other way. That person you are concerned about may be your son or daughter. Find encouragement in this firm confidence: The One who began a good work in your boy or in your girl will bring it to completion; He will finish the task. I repeat, that firm confidence in God's finishing what He started will bring back your joy.

I have mentioned joy stealers several times already. Perhaps this is a good place for me to identify three of these most notorious thieves at work today. All three, by the way, can be resisted by firm confidence, the kind of confidence we've been thinking about.

The first joy stealer is *worry*. The second is *stress*. And the third is *fear*. They may seem alike, but there is a distinct difference.

Worry is an inordinate anxiety about something that may or may not occur. It has been my observation that what is being worried about usually does not occur. But worry eats away at joy like slow-working acid while we are waiting for the outcome. I'll say much more about this thief in chapter 12.

Stress is a little more acute than worry. Stress is intense strain over a situation we cannot change or control—something out of our control. (Occasionally the safest place for something to be is out of *our* control.) And instead of releasing it to God, we churn over it. It is in that restless churning stage that our stress is intensified. Usually the thing that plagues us is not as severe as we make it out to be.

Fear, on the other hand, is different from worry and stress. It is dreadful uneasiness over the presence of danger, evil, or pain. As with the other two, however, fear usually makes things appear worse than they really are.

How do we live with worry and stress and fear? How do we withstand these joy stealers? Go back to Paul's words:

> For I am confident of this very thing, that He who began a good work in you will perfect it until the day of Christ Jesus.
>
> *Philippians 1:6*

Let me be downright practical and tell you what I do. First I remind myself early in the morning and on several occasions during the day, "God, You are at work, and You are in control. And, Lord God, You know this is happening. You were there at the beginning, and You will bring everything that occurs to a conclusion that results in Your greater glory in the end." And then? Then (and *only* then!) I relax. From that point on, it really doesn't matter all that much what happens. It is in God's hands.

I love the story of the man who had fretted for fifteen years over his work. He had built his business from nothing into a rather sizable operation. In fact, he had a large plant that covered several acres. With growth and success, however, came ever-increasing demands. Each new day brought a whole new list of responsibilities. Weary of the worry, the stress, and the fear, he finally decided to give it *all* over to God. With a smile of quiet contentment, he prayed, "Lord God, the business is Yours. All the worry, the stress, and the fears I release to You and Your sovereign will. From this day forward, Lord, You own this business." That night he went to bed earlier than he had since he started the business. Finally . . . peace.

In the middle of the night the shrill ring of the phone awoke the man. The caller, in a panicked voice, yelled, "Fire! The entire place is going up in smoke!" The man calmly dressed, got into his car and drove to the plant. With his hands in his pockets he stood there and watched, smiling slightly. One of his employees hurried to his side and said, "What in the world are you smiling about? How can you be so calm? Everything's on fire!" The man answered, "Yesterday afternoon I gave this business to God. I told Him it was His. If He wants to burn it up, that's His business."

Some of you read that and think, *That's insane!* No, that is one of the greatest pieces of sound theology you can embrace. Firm confidence in God means that it is in His hands. He who started something will bear the pressure of it and will bring the results exactly as He planned for His greater glory. How could a business burned to the ground be of glory to God? you may ask. Well, sometimes the loss of something very significant—perhaps something we are a slave to—is the only way God can get our attention and bring us back to full sanity. The happiest people I know are the ones who have learned how to hold everything loosely and have given the worrisome, stress-filled, fearful details of their lives into God's keeping.

We have seen that Paul remained joyful because he had great memories and because he lived with firm confidence.

Third, *he felt a warm affection toward his fellow believers.*

> For it is only right for me to feel this way about you all, because I have you in my heart, since both in my imprisonment and in the defense and confirmation of the gospel, you all are partakers of grace with me. For God is my witness, how I long for you all with the affection of Christ Jesus.
>
> *Philippians 1:7–8*

The term Paul uses for affection is, literally, the Greek word for "bowels." In the first century it was believed that the intestines, the stomach, the liver, even the lungs, held the most tender parts of human emotions. That explains why this joyful man would use "bowels" in reference to "affection." He says, in effect, "As I share with you my feelings, I open my whole inner being to you and tell you that the level of my affection is deep and tender." Too many people live with the inaccurate impression that Paul was somewhat cold and uncaring. Not according to this statement; in fact, quite the contrary! When he was with those he loved, Paul went to the warmest depths in conversation and affection.

If you have not yet read John Powell's *Why Am I Afraid to Tell You Who I Am?* you are missing a great experience. There is a section in the book that is worth a great deal of your time and attention. It is where the author presents the five levels of communication, which, he says, are like concentric circles—from the most shallow and superficial level (outer circle) to the deepest, most intimate level (smallest circle at the core).

Level five, the outer circle of superficiality, is the level he calls "cliché conversation."

> On this level, we talk in clichés, such as: "How are you? . . . How is your family? . . . Where have you been?" We say things like: "I like your dress very much." "I hope we can get together real soon." "It's really good to see you." [Which might really mean, "We may not see each other for a year, and I'm not going to sweat it."] . . . If the other party were to begin answering our question, "How are you?" in detail, we would be astounded. Usually and fortunately the other party senses the superficiality and conventionality of our concern and question, and obliges by simply giving the standard answer, "Just fine, thank you."[5]

That's cliché communication. Tragically, that is the deepest many people choose to go.

Level four is where we "report facts" about each other.

> We remain contented to tell others what so-and-so has said or done. We offer no personal, self-revelatory commentary on these facts, but simply report them.[6]

This is the realm of gossip and petty, meaningless little tales about others.

Level three leads us into the area of ideas and judgments. Rarely do people communicate at this deeper level. They are able, but they're not willing.

As I communicate my ideas, etc., I will be watching you carefully. I want to test the temperature of the water before I leap in. I want to be sure that you accept me with my ideas, judgments, and decisions. If you raise your eyebrows or narrow your eyes, if you yawn or look at your watch, I will probably retreat to safer ground. I will run for the cover of silence, or change the subject of conversation.[7]

Because this begins to get below the "skating" level, those who go to the depths of ideas and judgments are quite courageous.

Level two moves into "feelings."

If I really want you to know who I am, I must tell you about my stomach (gut-level) as well as my head. My ideas, judgments, and decisions are quite conventional. If I am a Republican or a Democrat by persuasion, I have a lot of company. If I am for or against space exploration, there will be others who will support me in my conviction. But the *feelings* that lie under my ideas, judgments and convictions are uniquely mine. . . .

It is these feelings, on this level of communication, which I must share with you, if I am to tell you who I really am.[8]

I would hazard a guess that less than 10 percent of us ever communicate on that "feeling" level. To my disappointment, I have discovered that husbands and wives can live for years under the same roof without reaching this level.

Level one is the most personal, intimate form of communication.

All deep and authentic friendships, and especially the union of those who are married, must be based on absolute openness and honesty. . . .

Among close friends or between partners in marriage there will come from time to time a complete emotional and personal communion.[9]

Such depth of communication, which Paul seems to have practiced on a regular basis, brings a satisfaction—and joy—like few things on earth. And when we are free to express our feelings this deeply, we have little difficulty offering up prayers that are meaningful and specific. Which is precisely what Paul mentions next.

SPECIFIC PRAYING

He names two things that are of equal importance: abounding love and keen discernment. Verse 9 says, "I pray that your love may abound." Verse 10, "I pray that you may approve things that are excellent."

To begin with, love—abounding love—needs to flow freely, somewhat like a river. But that river must be kept within its banks or it swells and overflows. And when that happens, disaster! If you have ever been in a region that has been flooded, you know the calamity floodwaters can create.

When love floods indiscriminately, we love everything, even the wrong things. Paul said it well. It is knowledge—*real* knowledge—and discernment—*keen* discernment—that keep love within its banks.

He concludes this opening paragraph on a high note when he writes of . . .

> . . . having been filled with the fruit of righteousness which comes through Jesus Christ, to the glory and praise of God.
>
> *Philippians 1:11*

What a prayer! I realize how much he loved those folks at Philippi when I read words like this.

When was the last time you wrote somebody and mentioned what you were praying for on their behalf? You and I may frequently pray for individuals, but seldom do we sit down and write a note, "Dear So-and-So, I want you to know I'm praying for these three things to take place in your life: one . . . two . . . three. . . ." Paul's model is worth duplicating. You quickly move beyond level five when you begin to communicate like that, and I challenge you to do it.

PRACTICAL APPLICATION

We begin to laugh again when we rest our full confidence in God. More specifically, according to what we have just read in Philippians 1:

- Confidence brings joy when we fix our attention on the things for which we are thankful.
- Confidence brings joy when we let God be God.
- Confidence brings joy when we keep our love within proper limits.

Even though we are just getting started, we have covered a lot of important territory. As I think about the practical side of all this, it occurs to me that joy is ours to claim. In fact, no one on earth can invade and redirect our life of joy unless we permit them to do so.

Hudson Taylor put it like this:

> It doesn't matter, really, how great the pressure is; it only matters *where the pressure lies*. See that it never comes *between* you and the Lord— then, the greater the pressure, the more it presses you to His breast.[10]

The pressure on you may be intense. A half-dozen joy stealers may be waiting outside your door, ready to pounce at the first opportunity. However, nothing can rob you of your hold on grace, your claim to peace, or your confidence in God without your permission. Choose joy. Never release your grip!

I have lived almost fifty-eight years on this old earth, and I am more convinced than ever that the single most important choice a follower of Christ can make is his or her choice of attitude. Only you can determine that. Choose wisely . . . choose carefully . . . choose confidently.

Earlier I paraphrased a poem by Ella Wheeler Wilcox. I want to close this chapter by quoting it as she wrote it.

The Winds of Fate

One ship drives east and another drives west
    With the selfsame winds that blow.
        'Tis the set of the sails
        And not the gales
    Which tells us the way to go.

Like the winds of the sea are the ways of fate,
    As we voyage along through life:
        'Tis the set of a soul
        That decides its goal,
    And not the calm or the strife.[11]

My advice? Set your sails for joy! You will never regret it.

3

*What a Way
to Live!*

*A*s a boy I spent my leisure hours in the evening listening to various radio shows. In those days before television, action-packed dramas, murder mysteries, and comedy programs—all on radio in the evening hours—were the ticket to adventure and imagination.

There were many to choose from in the 1940s: "The Green Hornet," "Captain Midnight," "Lum 'n' Abner," "The Lone Ranger," "Gang Busters," "Inner Sanctum," "Jack Armstrong (the All-American Boy)," "Fibber McGee and Molly," "Edgar Bergen and Charlie McCarthy," and my all-time favorite, "Mr. District Attorney." I listened to that program so often I memorized the announcer's words of introduction, which always concluded with "defender of our right to life, liberty, and the pursuit of happiness." I used to strut around the house mouthing those lines.

I didn't know it at the time but that part of the announcer's script was borrowed from Thomas Jefferson's immortal words in our nation's Declaration of Independence:

> We hold these Truths to be self-evident; that all Men are created equal, that they are endowed by their Creator with certain unalienable Rights; that among these are Life, Liberty, and the Pursuit of Happiness.

Those final words still intrigue me. One of our unalienable rights is to pursue happiness—to seek out a life of joy and to find peaceful satisfaction. For many, however, happiness is a forgotten pursuit. A dream that has died.

For the longest time I wondered why. Why has a joyful life, an attitude of happiness, eluded so many? Within the past few years I have come to realize why. It's because most people think that happiness is something that happens to them rather than something they deliberately and diligently pursue. Circumstances seldom generate smiles and laughter. Joy comes to those who determine to pursue it in spite of their circumstances.

A good reminder of this is the short story by G. W. Target entitled "The Window," which tells of two men, both seriously ill, who occupied the same small hospital room. One man was allowed to sit up in his bed for an hour each afternoon to help drain the fluid from his lungs. His bed was next to the room's only window. The other man had to spend all his time flat on his back.

The men talked for hours on end. They spoke of their wives and families, their homes, their jobs, their involvement in the military service, where they had been on vacation. And every afternoon when the man in the bed by the window could sit up, he would pass the time by describing to his roommate all the things he could see outside the window. The man in the other bed began to live for those one-hour periods where his world would be broadened and enlivened by all the activity and color of the outside world.

The window overlooked a park with a lovely lake, the man said. Ducks and swans played on the water while children sailed their model boats. Lovers walked arm in arm amid flowers of every color of the rainbow. Grand old trees graced the landscape, and a fine view of the city skyline could be seen in the distance. As the man by the window described all this in exquisite detail, the man on the other side of the room would close his eyes and imagine the picturesque scene.

One warm afternoon the man by the window described a parade passing by. Although the other man couldn't hear the band, he could see it in his mind's eye as the gentleman by the window portrayed it with descriptive words. Unexpectedly, an alien thought entered his head: *Why should he have all the pleasure of seeing everything while I never get to see anything?* It didn't seem fair.

As the thought fermented the man felt ashamed at first. But as the days passed and he missed seeing more sights, his envy eroded into resentment and soon turned him sour. He began to brood and he found himself unable to sleep. *He* should be by that window—that thought now controlled his life.

Late one night as he lay staring at the ceiling, the man by the window began to cough. He was choking on the fluid in his lungs. The other man watched in the dimly lit room as the struggling man by the window groped for the button to call for help. Listening from across the room, he never moved, never pushed his own button which would have brought the nurse running. In less than five minutes the coughing and choking stopped, along with the sound of breathing. Now there was only silence—deathly silence.

The following morning the day nurse arrived to bring water for their baths. When she found the lifeless body of the man by the window, she was saddened and called the hospital attendants to take it away—no words, no fuss. As soon as it seemed appropriate, the other man asked if he could be moved next to the window. The nurse was happy to make the switch, and after making sure he was comfortable, she left him alone.

Slowly, painfully, he propped himself up on one elbow to take his first look. Finally, he would have the joy of seeing it all himself. He strained to look out the window beside the bed.

It faced a blank wall.[1]

The pursuit of happiness is a matter of choice . . . it is a positive attitude we choose to express. It is not a gift delivered to our door each morning, nor does it come through the window. And it is certain that our circumstances are not the things that make us joyful. If we wait for them to get just right, we will never laugh again.

NEEDED: A POSITIVE MIND-SET

Since the pursuit of happiness is an inward journey, it might be helpful to see the two options available to us. Maybe if I put them into opposing columns, the contrast will leave a lasting impression.

Negative Mind-set	Positive Mind-set
• The need for certain things before there can be joy	• The need for virtually nothing tangible to be joyful
• A strong dependence on others to provide joy	• The ability to create one's own reasons for joy
• Focusing on joy as being "out there," always in the future . . . waiting for something to happen and thereby bring happiness	• Choosing joy now, making it a present pursuit . . . never waiting for everything to fall into place or for some "ship" to come in

These minds of ours are like bank vaults awaiting our deposits. If we regularly deposit positive, encouraging, and uplifting thoughts, what we withdraw will be the same. And the interest paid will be joy.

One day I came across a fat little book on a friend's desk, and the title grabbed my attention: *14,000 Things to Be Happy About.* As I thumbed through the contents, I realized that each of those 14,000 things was a happy thought, and each one could make the reader happy. However, there isn't one of those 14,000 things that will make us laugh again unless we give ourselves permission to do so. The secret lies in our mind-set—in the things we fix our minds on. As Paul wrote to the Philippians:

> And now, brothers . . . let me say this one more thing: Fix your thoughts on what is true and good and right. Think about things that are pure and lovely, and dwell on the fine, good things in others. Think about all you can praise God for and be glad about.
>
> *Philippians 4:8 TLB*

PAUL: A CLASSIC EXAMPLE OF HOW TO LIVE

Speaking of Paul, let me reintroduce you. This is the man who wanted to go to Rome as a preacher in order to testify of his faith before the emperor, Nero. Instead, he wound up in Rome as a prisoner. He was a Roman citizen with every right to appeal to Caesar and await an audience before him. Instead, he was illegally arrested in Jerusalem, misrepresented before the court, incorrectly identified as an Egyptian renegade, entangled in the red tape of political machinery, and finally granted a trip across the Mediterranean, only to encounter a storm and be shipwrecked. When he finally arrived in Rome, he was incarcerated and virtually forgotten for two years. If we looked up *victim* in the dictionary, Paul's picture should appear beside the word!

And yet he is the man who wrote his friends the most joyous letter in the entire New Testament.

Confident, Even Though a Victim

Read his words slowly and see if you find even a hint of resentment or negativism:

> Now I want you to know, brethren, that my circumstances have turned out for the greater progress of the gospel, so that my imprisonment in the cause of Christ has become well known throughout the whole

praetorian guard and to everyone else, and that most of the brethren, trusting in the Lord because of my imprisonment, have far more courage to speak the word of God without fear.

Philippians 1:12–14

Doesn't sound to me like a guy licking his wounds or attending a pity party in honor of himself. On the contrary, he reminds me of the man by the window in that hospital room, looking at a bleak, blank wall but determined to see the unseen. Sitting there with an iron cuff and chain on one arm, bound to a Roman soldier, Paul wrote of his circumstances as having turned out "for the greater *progress* of the gospel."

What a grand, positive statement! After all the man had been through, he considered the things most people would call setbacks as progress. The Greek term Paul selected is colorful. It was used in ancient times to describe a group of pioneer woodcutters who preceded an advancing army, clearing the way through an otherwise impenetrable forest of trees and underbrush. Paul viewed his circumstances as having cleared the way "for the greater progress of the gospel" of Christ to be released.

Instead of seeing the soldier on duty next to him as a galling restriction to the gospel, Paul saw him as a captive audience. What an opportunity to share Christ with one soldier after another, who would, in turn, take the same message back to the barracks so others in the elite praetorian guard might hear and believe. Instead of feeling frustrated and victimized, Paul laughed at the open window of unique opportunity offering numerous possibilities. Paul's joy was outrageous!

How can a person think like that? The answer is neither difficult nor complicated—but it all depends on the question we ask ourselves. Either we ask the negative: Why did this have to happen to me? Or we choose the positive: How has this resulted for some benefit God had in mind?

Like Joseph said many years earlier to his brothers who had ripped him off, "You meant evil against me, but God meant it for good" (Gen. 50:20). With that same positive mind-set, Paul chose to count his blessings rather than list his disappointments. Looking at everything from that perspective, he realized that what seemed a waste or a detour was, in fact, God's divine alchemy. What seemed like a delay had proven to be a divinely appointed opportunity for the message of Christ.

Joyful in Spite of Others

> Some, to be sure, are preaching Christ even from envy and strife, but some also from good will; the latter do it out of love, knowing that I am appointed for the defense of the gospel; the former proclaim Christ out of selfish ambition, rather than from pure motives, thinking to cause me distress in my imprisonment. What then? Only that in every way, whether in pretense or in truth, Christ is proclaimed; and in this I rejoice, yes, and I will rejoice.
>
> *Philippians 1:15–18*

Even back in that first-century era, in the earliest, dynamic days of the church, not everyone who spoke for God was a vessel of pure motive and guileless proclamation. Some deliberately tried to cause Paul distress. Spiritual dynamo though he was, Paul was not perpetually above pain or personal hurt. The man must have had a few dog days like the rest of us. In fact, I like the way Stuart Briscoe describes Paul:

> Whatever we may think of Paul, he was no alabaster saint on a pedestal. The statue and the pedestal are the products of our own lack of reality. The real Paul had a temper that got heated and feelings that got hurt. He was no computerized theological machine churning out inspired writings, but a very warm human individual who needed as much love as the next man, and then some.
>
> You can't hurt a computer's feelings or grieve a theological concept, but you can destroy a man. Paul was destructible, but he wasn't destroyed. And it wasn't for lack of somebody trying! The perspective that he had discovered allowed him to say that he didn't really mind what happened to him so long as nothing happened to stop the gospel, because in his understanding the message preached mattered more than the man preaching.[2]

A large part of learning how to laugh again is being broad-shouldered enough to let things be . . . to leave room for differences . . . to applaud good results even if the way others arrive at them may not be our preferred method. It takes a lot of grace not to be petty, but, oh, the benefits!

Let's see if I can paraphrase what the apostle is communicating here:

> So what if some preach with wrong motives? Furthermore, some may be overly impressed with themselves . . . and take unfair shots at me.

Who cares? What really matters is this: *Christ is being proclaimed* . . . and that thought alone intensifies my joy! All the other stuff, I leave to God to handle.

To do otherwise is to clutter our minds with judgmental and borderline legalistic thoughts which become joy stealers. They rob us of a positive mind-set. And what happens then? We become petty, cranky, grim people who must have everyone poured into our mold before we are able to relax.

It is important that we understand what is worth our passionate concern and what is not. Most things are not worth the trouble. But some things are. For example, when Paul wrote to the Galatians, he was so concerned about what was happening there that he exclaimed:

> But even though we, or an angel from heaven, should preach to you a gospel contrary to that which we have preached to you, *let him be accursed.* As we have said before so I say again now, if any man is preaching to you a gospel contrary to that which you received, *let him be accursed.*

> *Galatians 1:8–9 (italics mine)*

I don't think there is any disagreement . . . the man was hot! But here in Philippians Paul looked at what was going on around him and said, "So what?" The difference is that in Galatia the gospel was being tampered with—some people were preaching a false message of salvation. But in Philippi the truth was being proclaimed even though Paul, personally, was being attacked. When people mess with the message, they need to be rebuked, exposed, and corrected. But when they mess with the messenger, they need to be ignored. No big deal. Not even Paul wasted his time or burnt up a lot of energy nitpicking his way through all that. He was just thrilled that the gospel was being declared.

I have learned over the years that only a few things are worth going to the mat for, and those things always center on the clear gospel message and its surrounding truths. They do not have to do with defending oneself or trying to straighten out other preachers' motives or changing their style. Grace says to let them be. If Paul could shrug it off and say, "So what?" so should we. We will live a lot longer, and we'll start to laugh again.

Hopeful, Regardless of Uncertainties

> For I know that this shall turn out for my deliverance through your prayers and the provision of the Spirit of Jesus Christ, according to my earnest expectation and hope, that I shall not be put to shame in anything, but that with all boldness, Christ shall even now, as always, be exalted in my body, whether by life or by death.
>
> *Philippians 1:19–20*

Those are the words of a man whose image was secure and whose reputation was not in need of being protected, massaged, or defended. His mind was firmly fixed on essentials, so much so that nothing brought him anxiety. "Whether by life or by death," his focus was concentrated. He concerned himself only with things that mattered. For all he knew, death might be right around the corner.

That thought alone provides an excellent filtering system, enabling us to separate what is essential from what is not. As dear old Samuel Johnson once stated, "When a man knows he is to be hanged in a fortnight, it concentrates his mind wonderfully."[3]

Paul was hopeful, regardless of the uncertainties he faced. His quiet confidence is revealed in such phrases as "this shall turn out" and "my earnest expectation." In other words, what he was experiencing was not the end—things would turn out exactly as God directed. That brought the man a rush of mind-calming *peace.* And what may have temporarily brought him pain and discomfort would ultimately result in "Christ . . . exalted in my body." That gave him *hope.* Sandwiched between those two statements was his determination not to feel uneasy or ashamed: "I shall not be put to shame in anything." That brought him *confidence.*

Refusing to be crippled by other people's words, refusing to submerge himself in self-pity, and refusing to take criticism and attacks personally, Paul remained strong, positive, and sure. How could he be so strong? No question about that answer. The man was—

Contented Because Christ Was Central

> For to me, to live is Christ, and to die is gain.
>
> *Philippians 1:21*

This is a well-known statement in Christian circles. We have heard it frequently and quoted it often. Since it is so familiar, perhaps if we try to reword the verse we will discover how any other statement lacks the significance of the authentic words of Paul.

- For me to live is *money* . . . and to die is to leave it all behind.
- For me to live is *fame* . . . and to die is to be quickly forgotten.
- For me to live is *power and influence* . . . and to die is to lose both.
- For me to live is *possessions* . . . and to die is to depart with nothing in my hands.

Somehow, they all fall flat, don't they? When money is our objective, we must live in fear of losing it, which makes us paranoid and suspicious. When fame is our aim, we become competitive lest others upstage us, which makes us envious. When power and influence drive us, we become self-serving and strong-willed, which makes us arrogant. And when possessions become our god, we become materialistic, thinking enough is never enough, which makes us greedy. All these pursuits fly in the face of contentment . . . and joy.

Only *Christ* can satisfy, whether we have or don't have, whether we are known or unknown, whether we live or die. And the good news is this: Death only sweetens the pie! That alone is enough to make you laugh again!

The Living Bible states: "For to me, living means opportunities for Christ, and dying—well, that's better yet!" The New Testament in Modern English, J. B. Phillips's paraphrase, reads: "For living to me means simply 'Christ,' and if I die I should merely gain more of Him." The Good News Bible asks: "For what is life? To me, it is Christ. Death, then, will bring more."

What is the sum and substance of all this? The secret of living is the same as the secret of joy: Both revolve around the centrality of Jesus Christ. In other words, the pursuit of happiness is the cultivation of a Christ-centered, Christ-controlled life.

THREE THINGS TO REMEMBER

When Christ becomes our central focus—our reason for existence—contentment replaces our anxiety as well as our fears and insecurities. This cannot help but impact three of the most prevalent joy stealers in all of life.

1. He broadens the dimensions of our circumstances. This gives us new confidence. Chains that once bound and irritated us no longer seem so irksome. Our limitations become a challenge rather than a chore.

2. He delivers us from preoccupation with others. This causes our contentment level to rise. Other people's opinions, motives, and criticisms no longer seem all that important. What a wonderful deliverance!

3. He calms our fears regarding ourselves and our future. This provides a burst of fresh hope on a daily basis. Once fear is removed, it is remarkable how quickly peace fills the vacuum. And when we get those three ducks in a row, it isn't long before we begin to laugh again. What a way to live! Let me urge you not to let anything keep you from it.

Since it is your unalienable right to pursue happiness, I suggest that you *get with it* right away. For some, it is like breaking the spell you have been under for half your life, maybe longer. Won't that take a little extra energy? Probably. You're too tired to exert yourself . . . too tired to pursue *anything* more? Maybe this anonymous piece will help change your mind.

I'm Tired

Yes, I'm tired. For several years I've been blaming it on middle-age, iron poor blood, lack of vitamins, air pollution, water pollution, saccharin, obesity, dieting, underarm odor, yellow wax build-up, and a dozen other maladies that make you wonder if life is really worth living.

But now I find out, tain't that.
I'm tired because I'm overworked.

The population of this country is 200 million. Eighty-four million are retired. That leaves 116 million to do the work. There are 75 million in school, which leaves 41 million to do the work. Of this total, there are 22 million employed by the government.

That leaves 19 million to do the work. Four million are in the armed forces, which leaves 15 million to do the work. Take from that total the 14,800,000 people who work for the state and city governments and that leaves 200,000 to do the work. There are 188,000 in hospitals, so that leaves 12,000 to do the work. Now, there are 11,998 people in prisons. That leaves just 2 people to do the work. You and me. And you're standing there reading this. No wonder I'm tired.[4]

58

To you I say, *let go.* Let go of your habit of always looking at the negative. Let go of your need to fix everybody else's unhappiness. Let go of your drive to compete or compare. Let go of your adult children, especially your attempts to straighten out their lives. (I read recently that parents are never happier than their least-happy child. What a joy stealer!) Let go of all your excuses. And may I add one more? Let go of so many needless inhibitions that keep you from celebrating life. Quit being so protective . . . so predictable . . . so proper.

Far too many adults I know are as serious as a heart attack. They live with their fists tightened, and they die with deep frowns. They cannot remember when they last took a chance or risked trying something new. The last time they tried something really wild they were nine years old. I ask you, where's the fun? Let's face it, you and I are getting older—it's high time we stop acting like it!

Sooner than we realize, all of us will be looking out that window at a blank wall.

4

---

*Laughing Through
Life's Dilemmas*

*L*IFE GETS COMPLICATED.

I can't speak for you, but for me dilemmas are a regular occurrence. Some folks—at least from all outward appearances—seem to deal with life on a black-and-white basis. Stuff they encounter is either right or wrong. Not for me. Somehow I wind up in the gray area more often than not. Perhaps that's been your experience too.

If so, folks like us can appreciate the frustrations Charlie Brown frequently has, as portrayed in Charles Schulz's famous "Peanuts" cartoons. Like the one where Lucy is philosophizing and Charlie is listening. As usual, Lucy has the floor, delivering one of her dogmatic lectures.

"Charlie Brown," she begins, "life is a lot like a deck chair. Some place it so they can see where they're going. Others place it to see where they've been. And some so they can see where they are at the present."

Charlie sighs, "I can't even get mine unfolded!"

More than a few of us identify with Charlie. Life's dilemmas leave us unsettled and unsure. We find ourselves, like the old saying, between a rock and a hard place.

FAMILIAR DILEMMAS

Dilemmas have the potential of being some of life's most demanding joy stealers. Being stuck between two possibilities where a case could be made for going either way . . . ah, that's a tough call. We've all been there. I think they fall into at least three categories.

Volitional Dilemmas

A volitional dilemma occurs when we want to do two different things at the same time.

Young couples who have been married for two or three years, sometimes less, are often trying to finish their schooling, yet they are anxious to start a family. Which should they do? To start having children means extra financial pressure and an even greater struggle with time and energy drain. Yet to wait several years means that they may be in their thirties, and they would much rather begin parenting earlier than that. Which do they do?

Another volitional dilemma occurs when we find ourselves unhappy in our church. The problem is exacerbated by the fact that we have been members for many years and have our closest friends there. Do we stick it out and try to help bring about needed changes, which may not be too promising and could create ill feelings, or do we graciously declare our disagreement and leave?

Emotional Dilemmas

Emotional dilemmas are even more intense. They occur when we entertain contrary feelings about the same event.

Not too many months ago our younger son, Chuck, discovered that his longtime pet had a dreadful skin disease. Sasha, a beautiful white Samoyed, had been his dog for many years. To say they were close is to understate the inseparable bond between them. No matter what Chuck tried—and believe me, he tried everything—nothing helped. The dog became increasingly miserable. You have already guessed the dilemma. To provide Sasha relief meant putting her to sleep . . . an option so painful to Chuck he could scarcely discuss it.

If you think that one is difficult, how about dealing with a rebellious adult son or daughter? He or she has moved out of the home but is living a lifestyle that is both personally destructive and disappointing to you. It's obvious that some financial assistance could be put to good use. In fact, a request is made. Do you help or do you resist? Seems so objective, so simple on paper, but few dilemmas are more heartrending.

Geographical Dilemmas

Geographical dilemmas occur when we desire to be in two places at the same time. We love living where we have been for years, but moving would bring an encouraging financial advancement, not to mention the opportunity to cultivate new friendships and enjoy some much-needed changes. To leave, however, would be difficult because of the ages of the kids (two are older teenagers) and the longstanding relationships we have enjoyed at our church, in our neighborhood, and especially with our friends. We weigh both sides. Neither is ideal, yet both have their benefits—a classic geographical dilemma.

I am aware that there are some crossovers within these three categories, but by separating them we are able to see that each pulls at us and introduces numerous and deep feelings of strain, which can quickly drain our reservoir of joy. I might also add that being older and wiser does not mean we are immune to the problem. As Charlie Brown admitted, even seasoned veterans of life can find it difficult to get their deck chairs unfolded.

PAUL'S PERSONAL DILEMMA

All this brings us back to the man we have been getting to know better, Paul, a prisoner of Rome in his own house. We have watched him react positively to his circumstances, and we have cheered him on as he wrote words of encouragement to his friends in Philippi. Now we find ourselves identifying with his own personal dilemma to which he admits in the familiar words:

> For to me, to live is Christ, and to die is gain. But if I am to live on in the flesh, this will mean fruitful labor for me; and I do not know which to choose. But I am hard-pressed from both directions, having the desire to depart and be with Christ, for that is very much better; yet to remain on in the flesh is more necessary for your sake.
>
> *Philippians 1:21–24*

There can be no doubt: Paul's dearest friend, in fact his most intimate relationship on earth, was Christ. No one else meant more to him; therefore, the thought of being with Him brought Paul great joy.

His feelings could be those so beautifully summed up in an old gospel song:

> Jesus is all the world to me,
> My life, my joy, my all;
> He is my strength from day to day,
> Without Him I would fall. . . .

Jesus is all the world to me,
I want no better friend;
I trust Him now, I'll trust Him when
Life's fleeting days shall end.

Beautiful life with such a Friend;
Beautiful life that has no end;
Eternal life, eternal joy,
He's my Friend.[1]

When someone who is eternal and lives in heaven means that much to you, an inescapable dilemma is created: You want to be with Him! Now!! That explains why Paul did not hesitate to write "to die is *gain*." However, his work on earth was unfinished. God had more He wanted to do through His servant who was then under house arrest in Rome. Paul knew that, which was what caused the dilemma. He was between a rock and a hard place, or as he put it, "hard-pressed from both directions." And what were they?

1. "Having the desire to depart and be with Christ" (which he called "very much better"), and

2. "To remain on in the flesh . . . for your sake" (which he admitted, "is more necessary").

Let me spell all that out in even greater detail. To do so we need to analyze the benefits and the liabilities on both sides.

To Depart

The benefits? He would be with Christ instantly. He would be free of all earth's hassles and limitations, pain and frustrations. He would immediately experience uninterrupted peace and the joy of unending pleasure in the most perfect of all places.

The liabilities? He would be absent from those who needed him, which would seriously affect their spiritual growth. He would no longer be a witness to the Roman guards assigned to watch him or an encouragement to those who came to visit him. In addition, his missionary outreach to those who had not heard of Christ would instantly cease. Furthermore, all those whose cause he championed would be without a voice of authority and affirmation. As relieving as death may have seemed, it was not without its liabilities.

My mind rushes back to 1865 when our country was torn asunder by the Civil War. Abraham Lincoln stood in the gap as a source of strength when many grieving families were doubting and when helpless slaves were despairing. We can only imagine the pressure of that awful position. The photographs taken of the man before the war and during the conflict tell their silent story of a battle-weary warrior who must have longed for relief. Suddenly a shot was fired in Ford's Theater and everything changed. Our twelfth president finally knew peace as he had never known it before. Were there benefits? Yes! For him they were immediate and eternal. But the liabilities cannot be ignored: political chaos and rivalry among those in authority, heartbreaking sorrow added to an already grieving nation, and the voice of the African-American's most eloquent and powerful advocate forever silenced.

To Remain

If the apostle Paul remained on and continued his ministry, the benefits were obvious. He would have a hand in the spiritual growth of many, his role as mentor to the Philippians (and many others) would be sustained, and his vision for reaching a world without Christ would continue to rekindle the fires of evangelism everywhere he went. And we cannot forget the man's writing ministry. By remaining, his inspired pen would go on flowing.

The liabilities? He would remain absent from his heavenly home. The bonds of his imprisonment would not be broken, his pain would only increase, and his threatened future would intensify. And after all he had been through, who needed more? Bring on the relief!

You and I might think that the man was mature enough to hammer out this decision without too much of a struggle. After all, he was a strong and faithful soldier of the Christian faith, a wise counselor, and a spiritually minded man of God. Surely he could decide on his own. Yet, according to his own testimony, he admitted, "I do not know which to choose" (v. 22). Both made logical sense. Neither would be wrong . . . a real tossup. The Lord must lead, no question.

Horatius Bonar put his finger on the best solution to such a dilemma when he wrote:

> Thy way, not mine, O Lord,
>   However dark it be!
> Lead me by Thine own hand,
>   Choose out the path for me.

Smooth let it be or rough,
　　It will be still the best;
Winding or straight, it leads
　　Right onward to Thy rest.

I dare not choose my lot;
　　I would not, if I might;
Choose Thou for me, my God;
　　So shall I walk aright.

The kingdom that I seek
　　Is Thine; so let the way
That leads to it be Thine;
　　Else I must surely stray.

Take Thou my cup, and it
　　With joy or sorrow fill,
As best to Thee may seem;
　　Choose Thou my good and ill;

Choose Thou for me my friends,
　　My sickness or my health;
Choose Thou my cares for me,
　　My poverty or wealth.

Not mine, not mine the choice,
　　In things or great or small;
Be Thou my guide my strength,
　　My wisdom, and my all![2]

This is a timely moment for me to return to the greater theme of this book—joy. When we arrive at such dilemmas in life and are unable to decipher the right direction to go, if we hope to maintain our joy in the process, we must (repeat *must*) allow the Lord to be our Guide, our Strength, our Wisdom—our all! It is easy to read those words, but so tough to carry through on them. When we do, however, it is nothing short of remarkable how peaceful and happy we can remain. The pressure is on His shoulders, the responsibility is on Him, the ball is in His court, and an unexplainable joy envelops us. As viewed by others, it may even be considered outrageous joy.

To be sure, such an unusual method of dealing with dilemmas is rare—there aren't many folks willing to turn the reins over to God—and calls for humility, another rare trait among capable people. But it works!

The Lord is a Master at taking our turmoil and revealing the best possible solution to us.

As Peter once wrote:

> Humble yourselves, therefore, under the mighty hand of God, that He may exalt you at the proper time, casting all your anxiety upon Him because He cares for you.
>
> *1 Peter 5:6–7*

When we do that, He trades us His joy for our anxiety. *Such a deal!* As He then works things out and makes it clear to us which step to take next, we can relax, release the tension, and laugh again.

This is extremely hard for Type A personalities. If you happen to be more intelligent than the average person, it's even more difficult. And if you are the super-responsible, I-can-handle-it individual who tends to be intense and impatient, letting go and letting God take charge will be one of life's most incredible challenges. But I urge you, do it! Force yourself to trust Another who is far more capable and intelligent and responsible than you (or a thousand like you) ever could be. And in the meantime, enjoy!

Because I used to be much more driven and demanding (especially of myself), I would often search for things to read that would help me cool my jets. One excellent piece, written by a friar in a Nebraska monastery, has contributed more to my less-intense lifestyle than the author will ever know. I hope it will bring similar benefits your way.

> If I had my life to live over again, I'd try to make more
>   mistakes next time.
> I would relax, I would limber up, I would be sillier than
>   I have been this trip.
> I know of very few things I would take seriously.
> I would take more trips. I would be crazier.
> I would climb more mountains, swim more rivers, and
>   watch more sunsets.
> I would do more walking and looking.
> I would eat more ice cream and less beans.
> I would have more actual troubles, and fewer imaginary
>   ones.
> You see, I'm one of those people who lives life
>   prophylactically and sensibly hour after hour, day

after day. Oh, I've had my moments, and if I had
   to do it over again I'd have more of them.
In fact, I'd try to have nothing else, just moments, one
   after another, instead of living so many years
   ahead each day. I've been one of those people who
   never go anywhere without a thermometer, a hot-
   water bottle, a gargle, a raincoat, aspirin, and a
   parachute.
If I had to do it over again I would go places, do things,
   and travel lighter than I have.
If I had my life to live over I would start barefooted
   earlier in the spring and stay that way later in the
   fall.
I would play hookey more.
I wouldn't make such good grades, except by accident.
I would ride on more merry-go-rounds.
I'd pick more daisies.[3]

I know, I know. Just tolerating the idea of making mistakes and playing hookey and taking the time to pick daisies is tough for a lot of us. And
admittedly some have gone too far in this direction. It's one thing to err,
but when you wear out the eraser before the pencil, you're overdoing it.

Nevertheless, many need the reminder that life is more than hard
work and serious decisions and ultra-intense issues. I have often been
comforted with the thought that "He gives to His beloved even in his
sleep" (Ps. 127:2). How easy to forget that "God is for us" (Rom. 8:31)
and "richly supplies us with all things to enjoy" (1 Tim. 6:17). Some of
us need to read those statements every day until we really begin to believe them.

Well, did Paul experience God's leading? Was he ever removed from
the horns of his dilemma? Did he get his deck chair unfolded? You bet.
Read it for yourself.

And convinced of this, I know that I shall remain and continue with
you all for your progress and joy in the faith, so that your proud confidence in me may abound in Christ Jesus through my coming to you again.

Philippians 1:25–26

Somehow the Lord made it clear to Paul that His plan was to have
him remain and continue doing what he was doing. Though departing

would have brought the man instant relief and rewards for a job well done, he accepted God's decision and unselfishly pressed on.

A Spiritual Challenge

The closing words of Paul's opening chapter to his friends in Philippi are words of challenge—to them and to us.

> Only conduct yourselves in a manner worthy of the gospel of Christ; so that whether I come and see you or remain absent, I may hear of you that you are standing firm in one spirit, with one mind striving together for the faith of the gospel; in no way alarmed by your opponents—which is a sign of destruction for them, but of salvation for you, and that too, from God. For to you it has been granted for Christ's sake, not only to believe in Him, but also to suffer for His sake, experiencing the same conflict which you saw in me, and now hear to be in me.
>
> *Philippians 1:27–30*

What stands out to me is Paul's initial reminder that others are not responsible for our happiness. We are. "Whether I come and see you or remain absent," he expects to hear that they are together. What an important reminder!

So many live their lives too dependent on others. Such clinging vines draw most, if not all, of their energy from another. Not only is this unhealthy for the clinger, but it also drains too much energy from the clingee!

Paul would have none of that, and neither should we. Maturity is accelerated when we learn to stand firm on our own. There may be occasions when others play helpful roles during needy episodes of our lives, but those should be the exception rather than the rule. Codependent people are not joyful people.

Does this discount the need for close and harmonious relationships? Hardly. In fact, after encouraging a healthy independence, Paul turns the coin to the other side and suggests a need for balance: "with one mind striving together." Why? Because life includes tests, and some of those tests involve "opponents" who are not to alarm us. By striving together, we keep from being intimidated and frightened.

Great comfort comes when we realize that our striving is not an isolated series of battles fought one-on-one, but that we are fighting together against a common foe. There is a sense of camaraderie and support when we realize we are in the ranks of the faithful, a "mighty army" of those set apart by Christ, a force to reckon with.

After speaking at a church recently, I noticed an interesting sign as we were leaving the parking lot. It read:

YOU ARE NOW ENTERING
THE MISSION FIELD

Nice reminder. And even more encouraging, we enter it together. So we need to remember:

1. We are not alone.
2. We are promised the victory.
3. We are called (among other things) to suffer.
4. We are in good company when conflicts arise.

Paul reminds his friends at Philippi that their conflicts are the same as his conflicts. The Greek word translated *conflicts* here is the term from which we get our word *agony*. We agonize together just as we stand and strive for the gospel together. I gain strength from the thought that our sufferings and conflicts are on a par with Paul's. Agony is agony, pure and simple. It makes mature believers out of all of us. It also develops our spiritual muscles and gives us fresh courage to face whatever foe we may encounter. And let us never forget . . . our side ultimately wins!

In the early days of Christianity, a scoffer once inquired, "What is your Carpenter doing now?" And the answer of the unperturbed Christian was bold: "Making a coffin for your Emperor!"[4]

Never, ever forget that our role is twofold: not only "to believe in Him" (that's the delightful part), but also "to suffer for His sake" (the difficult part). That poses yet another dilemma, which would perhaps fall under a fourth category—the *practical* dilemma. We who love the Lord and faithfully serve Him, doing our best to live for His glory, occasionally find ourselves suffering for the cause rather than being rewarded for our walk. The dilemma: Do we run toward it or run from it?

Most in our day would consider anyone a fool who pursued anything but comfort and ease. But since when did the majority ever vote in favor of Christ? If this happens to be your current way of life, if suffering and difficulty have come your way because of your walk with Him, take heart. You are in good company. And some glorious day in the not-too-distant future, God will reward you for your faithfulness. You will have forgotten the pain of pressing on. And, like never before, you will laugh again.

OUR PERSONAL RESPONSE

Two final principles emerge from the things we have been thinking about in this chapter.

- Making right decisions amidst dilemmas forces us to rethink our priorities.

There is nothing quite like a dilemma to bring us back to the bed-rock of what we consider essential. Happy is the one who sets aside self-ish ambition and personal preference for God's will and way.

- Choosing right priorities forces us to reconsider the impor-tance of Christ in our lives.

There are many voices these days. Some are loud, many are persua-sive, and a few are downright convincing. It can be confusing. If you lis-ten long enough you will be tempted to throw your faith to the winds, look out for number one, let your glands be your guide, and choose what is best for you. Initially you will get a rush of pleasure and satisfaction, no question. But ultimately you will wind up disappointed and disillu-sioned.

Malcolm Muggeridge died in the fall of 1990. He had been a for-eign correspondent, newspaper editor, editor of *Punch* magazine, and a well-known television personality in Great Britain. As an adult, he fi-nally turned to Christ and wrote of his own dilemmas as a journalist-turned-believer. Among his works are *Jesus Rediscovered, Christ and the Media, Something Beautiful for God,* and his multivolume autobiography, *Chronicles of Wasted Time.* He frequently spoke and wrote of "feeling like a stranger" in the world.

In an interview a few years before his death, Muggeridge was asked if he would be willing to explain that feeling. His answer is worth repeating.

I'd very gladly do so, because I've thought about it often. In the war, when I was in North Africa, I heard some lieutenant colonel first use the phrase "displaced person." That phrase was very poignant to me. But it's also a very good definition of a person who's come to see that life is not about carnal things, or success, but is about eternity rather than time. . . . I don't really belong here, I'm simply staying here.[5]

Since I am committed to what is best for you, I am not going to suggest, "Oh, well, do whatever." I am going to challenge you to keep an eternal perspective, even though you are in the minority, even though you are surrounded by a host of success-oriented individuals who are urging you to ignore your conscience and grab all you can now. You want joy? You really want what is best? Simply consider yourself a displaced person and go God's way. His is the most reliable route to follow when life gets complicated. It will have its tough moments, but you will never regret it.

Some glorious day, trust me, you will look back on the dilemma that now has you so stressed out . . . and you will finally get your deck chair unfolded. You will then sit down on it and laugh out loud.

5

The Hidden Secret of a Happy Life

I HAVE BEEN WRITING A LOT about choosing joy and about cultivating a good sense of humor. On several occasions I have mentioned the value of one's attitude, which is the secret behind learning how to laugh again. Cultivating the right attitude, in my opinion, is absolutely crucial. Now let's take a deeper look at the subject of our attitude.

The dictionary on my desk defines attitude as "a manner of acting, feeling, or thinking that shows one's disposition . . . opinion, mental set." That means that how we think determines how we respond to others. As a matter of fact, I have found that my view of others is a direct reflection of my own "mental set."

> Our attitude toward the world around us depends upon what we are ourselves. If we are selfish, we will be suspicious of others. If we are of a generous nature, we will be likely to be more trustful. If we are quite honest with ourselves, we won't always be anticipating deceit in others. If we are inclined to be fair, we won't feel that we are being cheated. In a sense, looking at the people around you is like looking in a mirror. You see a reflection of yourself.[1]

Since I am a minister of the gospel, much of my time is spent studying the Bible and then sharing the things I have discovered. Lately my study has led me into the Gospel written by an ancient physician named Luke. As he began to do his research on the most incredible individual who ever lived on our planet, Dr. Luke was led to portray Jesus as a man. This portrayal provides fascinating information for anyone interested in Jesus' interpersonal relationships.

As I have pored over Luke's descriptions and observations, looking for insights into the Savior's life, I have been intrigued by His responses to others. How could any man be as patient as He was? How could He keep His cool under constant fire? How could He demonstrate so much grace, so much compassion, and at the same time so much determination? And when faced with the Pharisees' continued badgering and baiting, how could He restrain Himself from punching their lights out? As a man, He had all the emotions we have as human beings. What was it that gave Him the edge we so often lack? *It was His attitude.* To return to Webster's words, He acted and felt as He did because of His "disposition," His "mental set."

All this brings up a question: What is the most Christlike attitude on earth? Think before you answer too quickly. I am certain many would answer *love*. That is understandable, for He did indeed love to the uttermost. Others might say *patience*. Again, not a bad choice. I find no evidence of impatience or anxious irritability as I study His life. *Grace* would also be a possibility. No man or woman ever modeled or exhibited the grace that He demonstrated right up to the moment He breathed His last.

As important as those traits may be, however, they are not the ones Jesus Himself referred to when He described Himself for the only time in Scripture. I am thinking of those familiar words:

> Come to Me, all who are weary and heavy-laden, and I will give you rest. Take My yoke upon you, and learn from Me, for I am gentle and humble in heart; and you shall find rest for your souls. For My yoke is easy, and My load is light.

> *Matthew 11:28–30*

Did you catch the key words? "I am gentle and humble in heart," which might best be summed up in the one word *unselfish*. According to Jesus' testimony, that is the most Christlike attitude we can demonstrate. Because He was so humble—so unselfish—the last person He thought of was Himself.

ANALYZING UNSELFISHNESS

To be "humble in heart" is to be submissive to the core. It involves being more interested in serving the needs of others than in having one's own needs met.

Someone who is truly unselfish is generous with his or her time and possessions, energy and money. As that works its way out, it is demonstrated in various ways, such as thoughtfulness and gentleness, an unpretentious spirit, and servant-hearted leadership.

- When a husband is unselfish, he subjugates his own wants and desires to the needs of his wife and family.
- When a mother is unselfish, she isn't irked by having to give up her agenda or plans for the sake of her children.
- When an athlete is unselfish, it is the team that matters, not winning the top honors personally.
- When a Christian is unselfish, others mean more than self. Pride is given no place to operate.

As Isaac Watts wrote early in the eighteenth century:

> When I survey the wondrous cross
> On which the Prince of glory died,
> My richest gain I count but loss,
> And pour contempt on all my pride.[2]

What strange-sounding words! Not because they are archaic but because everyone today is so selfish—and we are never told by our peers to be otherwise. Ours is a day of self-promotion, defending our own rights, taking care of ourselves first, winning by intimidation, pushing for first place, and a dozen other self-serving agendas. That one attitude does more to squelch our joy than any other. So busy defending and protecting and manipulating, we set ourselves up for a grim, intense existence—and it is not a modern problem.

Greece said, "Be wise, know yourself."

Rome said, "Be strong, discipline yourself."

Religion says, "Be good, conform yourself."

Epicureanism says, "Be sensuous, satisfy yourself."

Education says, "Be resourceful, expand yourself."

Psychology says, "Be confident, assert yourself."

Materialism says, "Be possessive, please yourself."

Ascetism say, "Be lowly, suppress yourself."

Humanism says, "Be capable, believe in yourself."

Pride says, "Be superior, promote yourself."

Christ says, "Be unselfish, humble yourself."

When I write that last line, I find myself shaking my head and smiling. In our selfish, grab-all-you-can-get society, the concept of cultivating an unselfish, servant-hearted attitude is almost a joke to the majority. But, happily, there are a few (I hope you are one of them) who genuinely desire to develop such an attitude. I can assure you, if you carry out that desire, you will begin to laugh again—and I mean really laugh. It is the hidden secret of a happy life.

At our church in Fullerton, California, we are always looking for better ways to communicate with one another. It is easy for those of us in leadership to think everyone in the congregation is in the know when, in fact, they may be in the dark. We who stand up front and do the teaching and preaching can think everything we say is clear when it may not be. One method that has helped the congregation respond is the use of a tear-off section on our Sunday bulletins. Frequently folks will ask questions on these stubs or make a statement that helps them get a more realistic or complete view of something I have said from the pulpit.

Several Sundays ago someone wrote: "Chuck, I understand what you said today. I appreciate your commitment, and I believe every word of it. My problem is knowing how to do it!" I call that an extremely honest and humble response.

You may feel the same way about the things I have been saying regarding the value of maintaining an unselfish attitude. Perhaps you would even agree that unselfishness is the stuff of which Christlikeness is made . . . but how do we pull it off? You need to have it spelled out in more explicit, practical ways? Fair enough.

EXAMINING CHRISTLIKENESS

Let's go back to the little letter Paul wrote to his friends in Philippi. I think what he says regarding the attitude of unselfishness will help lift the fog of indefiniteness and enable us to get down to the nubbies of how to make it happen.

He begins this section with a plea:

> If therefore there is any encouragement in Christ, if there is any consolation of love, if there is any fellowship of the Spirit, if any affection and compassion, make my joy complete by being of the same mind, maintaining the same love, united in spirit, intent on one purpose. Do nothing from selfishness or empty conceit, but with humility of mind let each of you regard one another as more important than himself; do not merely look out for your own personal interests, but also for the interests of others.
>
> *Philippians 2:1–4*

These opening lines conclude with the theme of what is on his mind—"others." As we read Paul's initial plea, it is obvious that his major concern is that there not be disunity or conflict among his friends. It is as if he is pleading: Whatever else may happen, my friends, don't let a selfish attitude sneak in like a thief and steal your joy or interrupt your closeness.

What Is Needed?

Most of all, harmony is needed . . . a like-minded spirit with one another. I like the way The Living Bible renders the opening lines of this paragraph:

> Is there any such thing as Christians cheering each other up? Do you love me enough to want to help me? Does it mean anything to you that we are brothers in the Lord, sharing the same Spirit? Are your hearts tender and sympathetic at all? Then make me truly happy by loving each other and agreeing wholeheartedly with each other, working together with one heart and mind and purpose.
>
> *Philippians 2:1–2* TLB

What a wonderful way to live one's life! That "one heart and mind and purpose" suggests unity, a genuine Spirit-filled unselfishness that breeds strength and spreads cheer.

Is this suggesting uniformity? Does it mean we always have to agree on everything? Is that what harmony is all about? No. There is a difference between unity and uniformity. Uniformity is gained by pressure from without. The English word *uniformity* has within it the word *uniform*. We dress alike, look alike, sound alike, think alike, act alike. But that is neither healthy nor biblical. Unity comes from deep within. It is the inner desire to conduct oneself in a cooperative manner . . . to be on the same team, to go for the same objectives, for the benefit of one another.

As Harry A. Ironside said,

> It is very evident that Christians will never see eye to eye on all points. We are so largely influenced by habits, by environment, by education, by the measure of intellectual and spiritual apprehension to which we have attained, that it is an impossibility to find any number of people who look at everything from the same standpoint. How then can such be of one mind? The apostle himself explains it elsewhere when he says, "I think also that I have the mind of Christ." The "mind of Christ" is the lowly mind. And, if we are all of *this* mind, we shall walk together in love, considering one another, and seeking rather to be helpers of one another's faith, than challenging each other's convictions.[3]

Interestingly, Paul admits that their maintaining such a spirit of harmony would "make my joy complete." Harmony promotes happiness. If you question that, you've not worked at a place where disharmony reigns or lived in a home fractured by disunity. Joy cannot survive such settings. If we hope to laugh again, harmony needs to be restored.

How Is It Accomplished?

The question, I repeat, is how? How is it possible to pull off such an unselfish attitude when we find ourselves surrounded by quite the opposite? Let's look a little closer at what Paul wrote:

> Do nothing from selfishness or empty conceit, but with humility of mind let each of you regard one another as more important than himself; do not merely look out for your own personal interests, but also for the interests of others.

Philippians 2:3–4

As I consider his counsel, three practical ideas emerge that may help us cultivate an unselfish attitude.

First, never let selfishness or conceit be your motive. That's right, *never.* That is Paul's advice, isn't it? "Do *nothing* from selfishness or empty conceit" (emphasis mine).

Second, always regard others as more important than yourself. Though this is not a natural trait, it can become a habit—and what an important one!

Third, don't limit your attention to your own personal interests—include others. I think it was Andrew Murray who said: "The humble person is not one who thinks meanly of himself; he simply does not think of himself at all."

Some may try to dissuade you from what may appear to be an unbalanced, extremist position. They may tell you that anyone who adopts this sort of attitude is getting dangerously near self-flagellation and a loss of healthy self-esteem. Nonsense! The goal is that we become so interested in others and in helping them reach their highest good that we become self-forgetful in the process.

Go back momentarily to Paul's choice of words, "humility of mind." As we pursue this attitude (exalting Christ) and get involved in the same objective (being of help and encouragement to others), we set aside our differences (harmony) and lose interest in pleasing ourselves (unselfishness). Perhaps the closest we come to that is when we are forced to mutually endure hard times.

Martyn Lloyd-Jones, writing in England shortly after World War II, recalled the terror of the blitzkrieg bombing attacks of Hitler's Luftwaffe:

> How often during that last war were we told of the extraordinary scenes in air-raid shelters; how different people belonging to different classes, there, in the common need to shelter from the bombs and death, forgot all the differences between them and became one. This was because in the common interest they forgot the divisions and the distinctions. That is why you always tend to have a coalition government during a war; in periods of crises and common need all distinctions are forgotten and we suddenly become united.[4]

I have seen similar scenes out here in California in the midst of an awful fire that sweeps across thousands of acres, until finally those flaming fingers reach into a residential section. What happens? Immediately people pull together. They pay no attention to who makes what salary, which kind of car a person drives, or how much they might receive from their neighbor by helping out. Totally disregarding any benefit they personally might derive from their acts of heroism (usually nothing) and with no thought of personal danger, they "regard one another as more important" than their own possessions or safety. When we are forced to focus only on the help we can be to others in a time of crisis, we begin to demonstrate this Christlike attitude.

To be truthful about it, it does not always require a crisis. I have found that just having a large family—say, four or five kids—is enough to teach us how selfishness fouls up the works. I recall when Cynthia and I began to have children, I thought two would be perfect. "Alpha and Omega" . . . *ideal!* Along came our third . . . and not too many years later a fourth.

Now, you need to understand the kind of guy I am. I like my shoes spit-shined rather than stepped on and scuffed up. And I like my clothes hanging in the closet in an orderly and neat manner rather than drooled on and wrinkled up. And I really like milk in a glass on the table and not on the floor. I especially like a clean car with no fingerprints on the windows and no leftover school assignments spread across the floorboards.

So what does the Lord do to help broaden my horizons and assist me in seeing how selfish I am? Very simple: He gives me four busy kids who step on shoes, wrinkle clothes, spill milk, lick car windows, and drop sticky candy on the carpet. You haven't lived until you've walked barefoot across the floor in the middle of the night and stomped down full force on a jack . . . or a couple of those little Lego landmines. I'll tell you, you learn real quick about your own level of selfishness.

You see, this is not some deep, ethereal, or theological subject we're thinking about. Being unselfish in attitude strikes at the very core of our being. It means we are willing to forego our own comfort, our own preferences, our own schedule, our own desires for another's benefit. And that brings us back to Christ. Perhaps you never realized that it was His attitude of unselfishness that launched Him from the splendor of heaven to a humble manger in Bethlehem . . . and later to the cross at Calvary. How did He accept all that? Willingly.

CHRIST'S LIFE . . . BEFORE AND AFTER

A significant transitional statement appears at this juncture in Paul's words to the Philippians.

> Have this attitude in yourselves which was also in Christ Jesus. . . .
>
> *Philippians 2:5*

Christ Jesus, what a perfect example of an unselfish attitude! What Paul has been pleading for among his friends at Philippi, he illustrates in the person of Jesus Christ. In effect, he is saying, "You want to know what I'm getting at? You would like a 'for instance' to help you better understand what I mean by 'looking out for . . . the interest of others'? I call before you the perfect example: Christ Jesus."

Take a look at how He modeled this attitude:

> Have this attitude in yourselves which was also in Christ Jesus, who, although He existed in the form of God, did not regard equality with God a thing to be grasped, but emptied Himself, taking the form of a bond-servant, and being made in the likeness of men. And being found in appearance as a man, He humbled Himself by becoming obedient to the point of death, even death on a cross.
>
> *Philippians 2:5–8*

Everything that was involved in Jesus' becoming human began with an attitude of submission . . . a willingness to cooperate with God's plan for salvation. Rather than lobbying for His right to remain in heaven and continuing to enjoy all the benefits of that exalted role as the second member of the Godhead and Lord of the created world, He willingly said yes. He agreed to cooperate with a plan that would require His releasing ecstasy and accepting agony. In a state of absolute perfection and undiminished deity, He willingly came to earth. Leaving the angelic hosts who flooded His presence with adoring praise, He unselfishly accepted a role that would require His being misunderstood, abused, cursed, and crucified. He unhesitatingly surrendered the fellowship and protection of the Father's glory for the lonely path of obedience and torturous death.

Don't miss the steps downward:

1. He emptied Himself.
2. He took the form of a servant.
3. He was made in the likeness of humanity.
4. He humbled Himself by becoming obedient unto death.
5. He accepted the most painful and humiliating way to die—crucifixion.

Did He realize all this ahead of time? Of course. Was He aware that it would require such an extensive sacrifice? Without question. Did He do it all with a grim face and tight lips? Not at all. How do we know? You will find the answer to that tucked away in Hebrews 12:2,

> Fixing our eyes on Jesus, the author and perfecter of faith, who for the joy set before Him endured the cross, despising the shame, and has sat down at the right hand of the throne of God.
>
> *Hebrews 12:2*

Look at that! He saw those of us who would benefit from His sacrifice as "the joy set before Him." We're back to our theme—joy! He did not come to us grudgingly or nursing a bitter spirit. He came free of all that. While it was certainly not a pleasurable experience, He accepted His coming among us and His dying for us willingly and unselfishly.

And what ultimately happened? Read and rejoice!

> Therefore also God highly exalted Him, and bestowed on Him the name which is above every name, that at the name of Jesus every knee should bow, of those who are in heaven, and on earth, and under the earth, and that every tongue should confess that Jesus Christ is Lord, to the glory of God the Father.
>
> *Philippians 2:9–11*

Paul seems especially fond of compound superlatives. "God supremely exalted Him!" He was welcomed back with open arms. Heaven's applause was the supreme reward for His earthly sacrifice. Once again submission paid a rich dividend. We are told that two things occurred after the price for sin was paid:

1. God highly exalted Jesus Christ to the pinnacle of authority.
2. God bestowed on Him a name of highest significance: *Kurios Iesous Christos* . . . "Jesus Christ—Lord!"

No one else deserves that title. Only one is LORD. All knees will ultimately bow before Him. Above the earth? All angels will bow . . .

and all who have gone on before us. On the earth? Every living human being . . . those who love and worship Him and, yes, even those who deny and despise Him. One day in the future, all on earth will bow. Under the earth? The devil and his demonic forces along with those who have died without faith, unbelieving and lost.

> The lost will never be reconciled. Heaven and earth will eventually be filled with happy beings who have been redeemed to God by the precious blood of Christ. . . .
>
> But "under the earth" will be those who "have their part" in the outer darkness, the lake of fire. They flaunted Christ's authority on earth. They will have to own it in hell! They refused to heed the call of grace and be reconciled to God in the day when they might have been saved.[5]

A CONCLUDING ENCOURAGEMENT AND EXAMPLE

My emphasis in this chapter has been on the attitude that releases joy and launches it from our lips, the hidden secret of a happy life on earth—an attitude of unselfishness. My encouragement to you is that you not put it off until it is a little more convenient. Many will tell you that you will be taken advantage of if you begin to live for others or if you don't defend your rights and "get even." I offer the opposite counsel: God will honor your decision to demonstrate an attitude of humility. You will find that feelings of hate will be replaced with a relieving flood of peace and happiness. As Solomon has written, "When a man's ways are pleasing to the Lord, He makes even his enemies to be at peace with him" (Prov. 16:7).

Actually, it all begins with your knowing Jesus Christ in a personal way . . . and your allowing Him to take the blows of life for you. If you willingly do His will, you will find He gives you joy that even the angels of heaven cannot experience. Someday our voices will join the angelic host and together we will make great music! But our joy will outdo theirs.

There is an old gospel song I seldom hear anymore. Its chorus states what I'm trying to communicate:

> Holy, holy, is what the angels sing,
> And I expect to help them make the courts of heaven
>   ring;

But when I sing redemption's story, they will fold their
    wings,
For angels never felt the joys that our salvation
    brings.[6]

When we acknowledge that Jesus Christ is Lord and begin to release our cares, our disappointments, and our heartaches to Him, we not
only keep our equilibrium, we also keep our sense of humor. Joys multi-
ply when we have Someone to bear our burdens.

I mentioned earlier that I serve on the board of my alma mater. That
assignment carries with it many serious responsibilities but also several
joyous benefits. One of those has been the privilege of getting better acquainted with a fine group of Christian gentlemen who serve as colleagues on the same leadership team. One of them is a man I have
admired from a distance for many years—Tom Landry. As head coach
of the Dallas Cowboys for twenty-nine years and a member of the National Football League Hall of Fame, his record speaks for itself. But
what I find even more admirable are his character, his integrity, and his
humility. Now that I have gotten to know the man "up close and personal," my appreciation for him has only increased.

Most of us were surprised and disappointed at the way a new owner
of the Cowboys released Coach Landry from his position. I had the privilege of watching and listening to him during that time . . . even having a few personal conversations without microphones or television
cameras or news reporters nearby. He had ample opportunities to blast
the new management by criticizing their methods and defending himself. Not once—not a single time—following his forced resignation did I
hear an ugly remark or a blaming comment cross Tom Landry's lips. The
only response was something like, "You know, Chuck, a fellow in my
position has to realize it's going to be taken from him whether or not he
is ready for it to happen. It's just a matter of being willing to accept that."
Those are the unselfish words of a man who was told rather hurriedly to
clean out his desk and be on his way . . . after giving almost three de-
cades of his life to something he loved. Most others in his place would
have held a news conference within hours and blasted the new management unmercifully.

I have been with Coach Landry on numerous occasions since then.
We have had him at our church to speak to a gymnasium full of men
with their sons and friends. It has been delightful to observe a total

absence of bitterness in the man and, at the same time, the continued presence of a sense of humor and the joy of Christ. Personally, I am convinced his current attitude is a greater message to those to whom he speaks than all those years of success and championship seasons. It is reassuring to know that joy can endure hardship as long as that Christlike attitude of unselfishness is in place.

6

While Laughing, Keep Your Balance!

*D*IED, AGE THIRTY. BURIED, AGE SIXTY.

That's an appropriate epitaph for too many Americans. Mummification sets in on a host of young men and women at an age when they should be tearing up the track. All of us have so much more to offer for so much longer than we realize; it would boggle our minds if we could envision our full potential.

I came across an article way back in 1967 that I still return to on occasion. Entitled "Advice to a (Bored) Young Man," it communicates how much one person can contribute, if only—

Many people reading this page are doing so with the aid of bifocals. Inventor? *B. Franklin*, age 79.

The presses that printed this page were powered by electricity. One of the first harnessers? *B. Franklin*, age 40.

Some are reading this on the campus of one of the Ivy League universities. Founder? *B. Franklin*, age 45.

Some got their copy through the U.S. Mail. Its father? *B. Franklin*, age 31.

Now, think fire. Who started the first fire department, invented the lightning rod, designed a heating stove still in use today? *B. Franklin*, ages 31, 43, 36.

Wit. Conversationalist. Economist. Philosopher. Diplomat. Printer. Publisher. Linguist (spoke and wrote five languages). Advocate of paratroopers (from balloons) a century before the airplane was invented. All this until age 84.

And he had exactly two years of formal schooling. It's a good bet that you already have more sheer knowledge than Franklin had when he was your age.

Perhaps you think there's no use trying to think of anything new, that everything's been done. Wrong. The simple, agrarian America of Franklin's day didn't begin to need the answers we need today.

Go do something about it.[1]

After digesting a list like that, my immediate response is *Wow!* Who wouldn't be impressed? Examples like Benjamin Franklin are nothing short of fantastic. But they can also be frustrating.

I'm trying to put myself into the house slippers of a mother of four or five young children who does well to get dressed by eleven o'clock in the morning . . . or the recently unemployed forty-five-year-old husband and father who is spending his day on a job search, caught somewhere between pressure and panic. Furthermore, a lot of us do well just finding time to read about such inventions, to say nothing of spending the time it takes to discover them.

To keep things in balance it is helpful to remember the words of humorist Mark Twain: "Few things are harder to put up with than the annoyance of a good example."[2]

Admiration for a great person may inspire us, but it cannot enable us. Great potential notwithstanding, it is easy to feel overwhelmed.

WRONG RESPONSES TO RIGHT EXAMPLES

So what are the options frustrated folks take when exposed to great examples? To be sure, some *fake it.* Just polish the image and make a good appearance. Many make a career of doing that and never get caught. Others try to once and it backfires in spades. Back in 1990 a scandal hit the music industry. Milli Vanilli, who had won a Grammy Award for the album "Girl You Know It's True," finally had to confess it wasn't. They had lip-synced the entire recording, which resulted in the disgrace of having to return the Grammy.

To all that, Jimmy Bowen, president of Capitol Records, replied:

Ya have to remember that music is a mirror of the times. And when the mirror is close to what's happening, that's what sells. The times we live in are very plastic. There are a lot of phony things happening in people's daily lives. So Milli Vanilli is just playing the game.[3]

Another spokesperson in the same newspaper article added,

As technology allows music producers to use increasingly sophisticated electronic trickery to make albums and videos, the Milli Vanilli scandal will only repeat itself—unless audiences stop valuing image more than content.[4]

Another common technique when facing a great example is to *hurry the process*. I find that our generation, more than any in the past, wants more, *quicker*. "Don't slow me down by making me pay a price or go through some long and painful process. I don't want to wait until I'm in my fifties, sixties, or seventies. I want it now."

Regardless of your opinion of him, you have to agree that Liberace was one of the most popular entertainers of the latter half of the twentieth century. Recently I was interested to discover these comments on his style from the late pianist himself:

> "My whole trick," he says, "is to keep the tune well out in front. If I play Tschaikovsky, I play his melodies and skip his spiritual struggles. Naturally, I condense. I have to know just how many notes my audience will stand for. If there's time left over, I fill in with a lot of runs up and down the keyboard."[5]

There is another option, quite common in Christian circles. When faced with an example to whom we feel we cannot measure up, we *strive harder*. The old familiar song states this philosophy: "Striving to please Him in all that I do."

I ask you, is that the Christian life? If the answer is not faking it and if it is not hurrying things, is it striving hard for it? You want to live the rest of your life striving to please Him in all that you do? Some who are painfully honest will admit, "I'm doing my best. I'm trying. But I'm exhausted." Surely that's not God's plan.

CHRIST, OUR EXAMPLE

What may be true of other examples is not true of Jesus. Whether they be president or statesman, inventor or novelist, athlete or artist, all other great examples may inspire, but they cannot enable. They may motivate us, but they have no power to change us. There is nothing of Ben Franklin left over that can make you or me the inventor he was. But when it comes to Christ, things are different. He says, in effect, "You want to live My life? Here is My power." Lo and behold, He strengthens us within. "You want to please My heavenly Father? Here's My enablement." And He enables us by His Spirit.

Having failed far more than I have succeeded at many of my dreams, I find that very encouraging. And perhaps you would have to say the same thing. Having been swamped by sin all our lives, struggling to find our way to the top of the water to breathe, we can find great hope in the ability He gives us not only to breathe but to swim freely. You see, Christ not only lived an exemplary life, He also makes it possible for us to do the same. He gives us His pattern to follow *without* while at the same time providing the needed power *within*. And guess what that makes us able to do? Laugh again!

I mean it in the right sense when I say that for years Jesus has made me laugh. Because we have His example to follow and His power to pull it off, you and I no longer have to fake it or hurry it or strive for it. Once He gets control of our minds, the right attitudes bring about the right actions.

LIFE, OUR CHALLENGE

Having established the preeminent role Christ plays in our minds, we need to see how all that works its way out in our lives. Which brings us back to the little letter Paul wrote his friends in Philippi. In this choice missive promoting outrageous joy, he spells out the importance of keeping ourselves balanced as we take on the challenges of life. In doing this he specifies three of the most significant areas we must deal with:

- Balancing purpose and power (2:12–13)
- Balancing attitude and action (2:14–16)
- Balancing seriousness and joy (2:17–18)

Let's take them in that order.

Balancing Purpose and Power

So then, my beloved, just as you have always obeyed, not as in my presence only, but now much more in my absence, work out your salvation with fear and trembling; for it is God who is at work in you, both to will and to work for His good pleasure.

Philippians 2:12–13

96

We need to keep in mind that Paul is writing to Christians ("my beloved"), so obviously these words have nothing to do with his readers' becoming Christians—they already are. Therefore, the idea of working out one's salvation must be referring to living out one's faith—carrying it out correctly. In other words, we, as God's people, are charged with the importance of obedience. Just as Christ, our example, was "obedient to the point of death" (2:8), so we are to carry out our purpose with equal diligence.

Interestingly, the word translated "work out" was the same Greek term popularly used for "working a mine" or "working a field." In each case there were benefits that followed such diligence. The mine would yield valuable elements or ore . . . the field would yield crops. Paul's point is clear: By working out our salvation, we bring the whole purpose to completion . . . we carry out our reason for existence. So let's not stop short!

When a musician has a fine composition placed before her, that music is not the musician's masterpiece; it is the composer's gift to the musician. But it then becomes the task of the musician to work it out, to give it sound and expression and beauty as she applies her skills to the composition. When she does, the composition reaches its completed purpose and thrills the hearts of her listeners.

When we become ill, we go to a physician. He diagnoses our ailment and prescribes the proper treatment. He hands us a small slip of paper upon which he has written the correct prescription, and we take it to the pharmacist who fills that prescription and gives us the medication. So far, everything has been done for us—diagnosis, prescription, medication. It now becomes our responsibility to follow the doctor's orders exactly as stated. By working out the process we enjoy the benefits of the physician's and pharmacist's contributions to our health. We recover.

Spiritually speaking, the ultimate goal or purpose of our lives is "His good pleasure." Our lives are to be lived for God's greater glory—not our own selfish desires.

Are we left to do so all alone? Is it our task to gut it out, grit our teeth, and do His will? Not at all. Here's the balance: *God is at work in us!* He is the one who gives us strength and empowers our diligence. As He pours His power into us, we do the things that bring Him pleasure. Take special note that His pleasure (not ours), His will (not ours), His glory (not ours) are what make life meaningful. And therein lies a potential conflict, since most of us prefer to have things go our way. All this brings us back to that famous A-word—attitude.

Balancing Attitude and Action

> Do all things without grumbling or disputing; that you may prove yourselves to be blameless and innocent, children of God above reproach in the midst of a crooked and perverse generation, among whom you appear as lights in the world, holding fast the word of life, so that in the day of Christ I may have cause to glory because I did not run in vain nor toil in vain.
>
> *Philippians 2:14–16*

The first part of Paul's counsel here represents the negative side and the last part, the positive. The two provide another needed balance.

Negatively, watch your attitude! A bad attitude reveals itself from two sides: something we do alone—"grumbling"—and something we do when we are with others—"disputing." Both of these joy stealers need to be exposed.

What exactly is grumbling? It is not loud, boisterous grousing but rather low-toned, discontented muttering. It is negative, muted comments, complaining and whining. Disputing, however, is vocal, ill-natured argumentation . . . verbal expressions of disagreement that stir up suspicion and distrust, doubt and other disturbing feelings in others.

Some folks, like the British novelist J. B. Priestly (by his own admission), spread negative germs by their bad attitudes and acrid tongues. He once declared:

> I have always been a grumbler. I am designed for the part—sagging face, weighty underlip, rumbling, resonant voice. Money couldn't buy a better grumbling outfit.[6]

Ever been around a sourpuss like that? We all have. And even when we try to resist being influenced by such negativism, we find some of it rubbing off. How unfair to pass around the poison of pessimism! But it happens every day, and it steals our joy. It creates an atmosphere of wholesale negativism where nothing but the bad side of everything is emphasized. It is enough to make you scream!

I couldn't help but smile when I read Barry Siegel's satirical article "World May End with a Splash" in the *Los Angeles Times*. In a light-hearted way it shows how ridiculous it is to let negativism take charge:

> Alarmists, worrying about such matters as nuclear holocaust and pes-ticide poisoning, may be overlooking much more dire catastrophes. Con-sider what some scientists predict: If everyone keeps stacking *National Geographics* in garages and attics instead of throwing them away, the magazine's weight will sink the continent 100 feet some time soon and we will all be inundated by the oceans.
>
> If the number of microscope specimen slides submitted to one St. Louis Hospital laboratory continues to increase at its current rate, that metropolis will be buried under 3 feet of glass by the year 2024. If beachgoers keep returning home with as much sand clinging to them as they do now, 80 percent of the country's coastline will disappear in 10 years. . . .
>
> [It has also been reported] that pickles cause cancer, communism, airline tragedies, auto accidents and crime waves. About 99.9% of cancer victims had eaten pickles some time in their lives. . . . So have 100% of all soldiers, 96.8% of Communist sympathizers and 99.7% of those in-volved in car and air accidents. Moreover those born in 1839 who ate pick-les have suffered 100% mortality rate and rats force-fed 20 pounds of pickles a day for a month ended up with bulging abdomens and loss of appetite.[7]

Crazy stuff, but isn't that the way it is when grumbling and com-plaining are allowed to run wild? Those who hope to laugh again—those who genuinely wish to get beyond the doomsday mentality that pervades so much of today's newscasts, shop talk, and run-of-the-mill conversa-tions among Christians and non-Christians alike—must learn to "do all things without grumbling or disputing." Verbal pollution takes a heavy toll on everyone. Furthermore, who gave anyone the right to pollute the air with such pessimism? I agree with the person who said:

> We have no more right to put our discordant states of mind into the lives of those around us and rob them of their sunshine and brightness than we have to enter their houses and steal their silverware.[8]

I would love to hurry on past this subject, but I'd be less than hon-est if I left the impression that this is never my problem. I must confess that I, too, occasionally battle with negativism. When I do, it is usually my wife Cynthia who suffers the brunt of it. She has been pretty patient to endure it for more than thirty-seven years. I'm not as bad as I used to be, but every once in a while it surfaces.

Some of my readers know the ongoing debate that Cynthia and I have about bougainvillea. Years ago she really wanted us to plant several containers of bright red bougainvillea. It is a wonderful plant if you look at just the blossoms. But hidden within the plant are thorns . . . I mean those suckers are wicked! When Cynthia looks at bougainvillea, she sees only blossoms. When I look at the plant, I see only thorns. Unfortunately, there is a house not far from our home with a spectacular blooming bougainvillea climbing off the roof out front. Whenever we pass that house, Cynthia likes to drive a little slower and enjoy the blossoms. At certain times of the year she will point out, "Look how beautifully that bougainvillea is blooming." I will usually respond, without looking, "Do you realize the size of its thorns? I mean they are big . . . and they grow all over that plant. You may not see them, but if you walk close enough, you may never get free. It could catch you and hold you for half a morning."

Cynthia isn't convinced. She even said to me on one occasion, "Do you realize, honey, that every time—I mean *every time*—I mention bougainvillea, you grouse about the thorns?" (I might add that that conversation led to a dispute between us.)

In a lighthearted moment several years ago, I revealed our ongoing disagreement from the pulpit of our church, and much to my chagrin some anonymous soul sent us ten five-gallon containers of bougainvillea. I never told my wife, however, and we still have not planted bougainvillea. It is not God's will that we have bougainvillea. Too many thorns. Cynthia says she is confident that heaven will be full of bougainvillea. Since heaven is a perfect place, I maintain they would have to be a thornless species.

Positively, *prove that you are different!*

. . . prove yourselves to be blameless and innocent, children of God above reproach in the midst of a crooked and perverse generation, among whom you appear as lights in the world, holding fast the word of life, so that in the day of Christ I may have cause to glory because I did not run in vain nor toil in vain.

Philippians 2:15–16

Ours is a world of crooks and perverts, says my friend Ray Stedman, when he teaches this passage of Scripture. He is right. And since that is true, we need to model lives that are not like the majority. A positive attitude makes a major statement in our "crooked and perverse generation." We don't need to shout it out or make a superpious appearance; just don't grumble or dispute.

Paul goes further as he identifies four startling differences between those who know Christ and those who don't. These four descriptive words make all the difference in the world. Unlike our unbelieving friends, we are to be:

1. *Blameless.* This suggests a purity of life that is both undeniable and unhypocritical . . . free of defect.

2. *Innocent.* This means unmixed and unadulterated . . . inexperienced in evil . . . untainted in motive . . . possessing integrity.

3. *Above reproach.* This description is used of sacrificial lambs offered on altars and means free of blemish.

4. *Lights.* Actually the term used here means "luminaries," meaning we are to shine like stars surrounded by darkness.

In fact, Paul goes on to say that as we shine like stars, we are "holding fast the word of life."

Where did we pick up the mistaken idea of "This little light of mine, I'm gonna let it shine"? We are never called "little lights" in the Bible . . . we are *stars*. Bold, blazing, light-giving stars! This aching, hurting, confused world of lost humanity exists in dark rooms without light. Let it shine, fellow star! Why? Jesus answers that question in the sermon He delivered on the mountain:

> Let your light shine before men in such a way that they may see your good works, and glorify your Father who is in heaven.
>
> *Matthew 5:16*

No need to shout, scream, or make a scene. Just shine. Just live a life free of grumbling and disputing. The difference will jolt them awake. Furthermore, we will not live our lives "in vain." And speaking of that, Paul declares that he "did not run in vain nor toil in vain." What a claim to make as one begins to get up in years: No wasted effort!

My good friend David Roper, a pastor in Boise, Idaho, was, for a number of years, associate pastor alongside Ray Stedman at Peninsula Bible Church. You may know and appreciate Dave's ministry and writings, as I certainly do. Many years ago while Dave was ministering in Palo Alto on the campus of Stanford University, he arrived early one morning before the Bible study group had gathered. He was standing near an open courtyard and noticed an overgrown area where some kind of stonework was buried beneath vines and overgrowth. Dave's curiosity led him to go over and pull the vines away and tear back some of the overgrowth. When he did, he uncovered an ornate, hand-sculptured, stone birdbath. Though beautiful and unique, it was no longer being used. All the work the sculptor had put into that birdbath was wasted. When he saw this, Dave said he was moved to pray, "Lord, keep me from wasted effort. Don't let me build birdbaths with my life."

You and I can "run in vain and toil in vain" so easily. And afterward, looking back on that life, we will have to live with those vivid memories and feelings, "in vain . . . all wasted effort." We may not be in the category of a Ben Franklin, but we have the power of Jesus Christ working within us to give us all that is needed to make whatever impact He would have us make.

Balancing Seriousness and Joy

Not allowing our lives to become useless birdbaths—that is an extremely serious thought. But Paul gets even more serious:

> But even if I am being poured out as a drink offering upon the sacrifice and service of your faith, I rejoice and share my joy with you all. And you too, I urge you, rejoice in the same way and share your joy with me.
>
> *Philippians 2:17–18*

I find another word picture worth analyzing here. Paul speaks of the possibility of his "being poured out as a drink offering." This picture is drawn from a practice the pagans had of pouring out a chalice of wine before or after their meals in honor of the gods they worshiped. It was called a libation and was poured out either to gain the favor of or soften the anger of their gods.

Paul's thought is a serious analogy: I may never get out of this situation alive. It may be God's will that my life be poured out as a libation.

Even if that is so, even if it means the end of my life, this pouring out of my days on your behalf is worth every moment. Even if this imprisonment is my last, I rejoice!

I want to underscore something about Paul here: *There lived a balanced man.* While imagining that he might be living his final days, the single most serious thought a person could have, he was still able to rejoice. He refused to focus only on the dark side. He refused to let even the possibility of immediate and sure death steal his joy. In fact, he urged his friends to "rejoice in the same way."

Amazing! We cannot get through any major section of this letter without returning to Paul's themes of joy, rejoicing, and laughter. What a balanced man! A seasoned and scarred veteran missionary, yet all the while possessing a keen sense of humor. I have known a few men and women like that in my lifetime, and they never fail to bring refreshment and new hope. To remain superserious all the time and fill one's mind with only the harsh and painful realities of life keeps the radius of our perspective too tight and the tunnel of our hope too long. Paul refused to do that, and he wanted to make sure his Philippian friends followed suit.

Virtually every day I can find at least one thing to laugh about. There may be a few exceptions, but those days are rare indeed. Even though pain or difficult circumstances (Paul had both on a daily basis) may be our faithful companions, we encounter something each day that can prompt a chuckle or, for that matter, a hearty burst of laughter. And besides, it's healthy!

Experts tell us that laughter not only makes our serious lives lighter, but laughter also helps control pain in at least four ways: (1) by distracting our attention, (2) by reducing the tension we are living with, (3) by changing our expectations, and (4) by increasing the production of endorphins, the body's natural painkillers.[9] Laughter, strange as it may seem, turns our minds from our seriousness and pain and actually creates a degree of anesthesia. By diverting our attention from our situation, laughter enables us to take a brief excursion away from the pain.

Sometimes it is not literal pain but a too-serious mind-set. When our world begins to get too serious, we need momentary interruptions of just plain fun. A surprising day off, a long walk in the woods, a movie, an enjoyable evening relaxing with a friend over a bowl of popcorn, a game of racquetball or golf—these diversions can make all the difference in our ability to cope with life's crushing demands. We need to give ourselves permission to enjoy various moments in life even though all of life is not in perfect order. This takes practice, but it's worth the effort. It helps break guilt's stranglehold on us.

> Some saints can't enjoy a meal because the world is starving. They can't joyfully thank God for their clothing and shelter because the world is naked and homeless. They are afraid to smile because of the world's sadness. They're afraid to enjoy salvation because of the world's lost ones. They can't enjoy an evening at home with their families because they feel they ought to be out 'saving souls'. They can't spend an hour with an unforgiven one without feeling guilty if they haven't preached a sermon or manifested a 'sober Christian spirit'. They know nothing of balance. And they're miserable because of it. They have no inner incentive to bring people into a relationship with Christ which would make them feel as miserable as they themselves feel. They think the Gospel is 'good news' until you obey it and then it becomes an endless guilt-trip.
>
> There are leisure centres, sports centres, sewing centres, diet centres, entertainment centres and guilt centres. This last group is usually called 'Churches'. The endless harping on the string of guilt is part of the reason for all this gloom and uncertainty.[10]

SELF, OUR BATTLE

I want to close this chapter on balance with a warning. Old habits are terribly hard to break. Down inside of you is a voice that continues to nag you as you read these pages. It is saying, "No, no, no, No, NO!" As soon as you attempt to bring some necessary balance into your life, you are going to have a fight on your hands. After all, self has had its way for years. Giving you the freedom to laugh again and bring some needed joy into your life is not on self's agenda.

No matter. This invisible master needs to be brought back under the authority of Christ if you ever hope to laugh again. A life lived under the dominion of self is both unsatisfying and unproductive.

Here are a couple of suggestions for getting started:

1. Control self's urges to take the credit. When self reigns supreme, it lives for moments of personal gratification. Wean it away. Once you are able to see how out of balance you have become, you will have fresh strength to control its urges. Self needs to be bucked off its high horse.

John Wooden, former coach of the UCLA Bruins basketball team for so many national championship seasons, gives this helpful advice:

Talent is God-given, be humble;
Fame is man-given, be thankful;
Conceit is self-given, be careful.[11]

2. Conquer self's tendency to take charge. The longer you live the more you will realize the value of having Christ call the shots in your life. Not self, Christ. But that age-old battle will continue. Self wants to gain the mastery and convince you that it is a reusable source of energy. It is not. Self cannot be trusted. Any day you forget that and turn the controls over to self will be another day you will operate on strictly human energy, and you will lack the Spirit's power.

Back in the fall of 1990, I had an opportunity to minister to the military servicemen and women in Mannheim, Germany, along with two colleagues, Paul Sailhamer and Howie Stevenson. Since that area of Europe is Martin Luther Country, during our off-hours we visited the reformer's old haunts, the places he lived and wrote and served his Lord. There is something deeply invigorating about looking at a historic wall black with age or walking through a stone courtyard or standing in an ancient cathedral where a great man or woman once made history. It is as if that voice still speaks from the woodwork or that inimitable shadow still darkens the wall.

We stood where Luther stood at Worms when he defended himself before the Roman Church, a history-making moment known today as the Diet of Worms. There the most significant officials of the church had gathered to hear the German monk's declaration of the doctrine of salvation by grace alone—*Sola Fide.* In that emotion-charged moment he stood alone, unintimidated and resolute.

Just before Luther's audience with the pope, the prelates, the cardinals, and the emperor, a friend moved alongside the maverick monk and asked, "Brother Martin, are you afraid?" Luther responded with a marvelous answer: "Greater than the pope and all his cardinals, I fear most that great pope, self."[12]

And so should we. But if we hope to bring things back into balance—if we hope to change our habits of negative thinking, which leads to grumbling and a too-serious mentality—we'll have to dethrone this master and give the right Master His rightful place over our lives. Not until we do, I remind you, will we begin to laugh again.

7

Friends Make Life More Fun

*I*F I HAVE LEARNED ANYTHING during my journey on Planet Earth, it is that people need one another. The presence of other people is essential—caring people, helpful people, interesting people, friendly people, thoughtful people. These folks take the grind out of life. About the time we are tempted to think we can handle things all alone—boom! We run into some obstacle and need assistance. We discover all over again that we are not nearly as self-sufficient as we thought.

In spite of our high-tech world and efficient procedures, people remain the essential ingredient of life. When we forget that, a strange thing happens: We start treating people like inconveniences instead of assets.

This is precisely what humorist Robert Henry, a professional speaker, encountered one evening when he went to a large discount department store in search of a pair of binoculars.

As he walked up to the appropriate counter he noticed that he was the only customer in the store. Behind the counter were two salespersons. One was so preoccupied talking to "Mama" on the telephone that she refused to acknowledge that Robert was there. At the other end of the counter, a second salesperson was unloading inventory from a box onto the shelves. Growing impatient, Robert walked down to her end of the counter and just stood there. Finally, she looked up at Robert and said, "You got a number?"

"I got a what?" asked Robert, trying to control his astonishment at such an absurdity.

"You got a number? You gotta have a number."

Robert replied, "Lady, I'm the only customer in the store! I don't need a number. Can't you see how ridiculous this is?" But she failed to see the absurdity and insisted that Robert take a number before agreeing to wait on him. By now, it was obvious to Robert that she was more interested in following procedures than helping the customer. So, he went to the take-a-number machine, pulled number 37 and walked back to the salesperson. With that, she promptly went to her number counter, which revealed that the last customer waited on had been holding number 34. So she screamed out, "35! . . . 35! . . . 36! . . . 36! . . . 37!"

"I'm number 37," said Robert.

"May I help you?" she asked, without cracking a smile.

"No," replied Robert, and he turned around and walked out.[1]

Now, there's a lady who's lost sight of the objective. I might question whether something like that ever happened if I had not experienced similar incidents in my own life. How easily some get caught up in procedures and lose sight of the major reason those procedures were established in the first place. Without people there would be no need for a store. Without people, who cares how efficient a particular airline may be? Without people a school serves no purpose, a row of houses no longer represents a neighborhood, a stadium is a cold concrete structure, and even a church building is an empty shell. I say again: We need each other.

A while back I came across the following piece that addresses this very subject with remarkable insight:

How Important Are You?

More than
you think.
A rooster
minus a hen
equals
no baby chicks.
Kellogg minus
a farmer
equals
no corn flakes.
If the nail
factory closes,
what good is the
hammer factory?
Paderewski's
genius wouldn't have
amounted to much
if the

piano tuner
hadn't shown up.
A cracker maker
will do better
if there's a
cheesemaker.
The most skillful
surgeon needs
the ambulance driver
who delivers the
patient.
Just as Rodgers
needed Hammerstein
you need someone
and someone
needs you.[2]

Since none of us is a whole, independent, self-sufficient, super-capable, all-powerful hotshot, let's quit acting like we are. Life's lonely enough without our playing that silly role.

The game's over. Let's link up.

People are important to each other. Above all, people are important to God. Which does not diminish His authority and self-sufficiency at all. The creation of humanity on the sixth day was the crowning accomplishment of the Lord's Creation handiwork. Furthermore, He put into mankind His very image, which He did not do for plant life or animals, birds, or fish. It was for the salvation of humanity, not brute beasts, that Christ came and died, and it will be for us that He will someday return. The major reason I am involved in a writing ministry and a broadcasting ministry and a church ministry is that people need to be reached and nurtured in the faith. This could be said of anyone serving the Lord Christ.

Couldn't God do it all? Of course, He is God—all-powerful and all-knowing and all-sufficient. That makes it all the more significant that He prefers to use us in His work. Even though He could operate completely alone on this earth, He seldom does. Almost without exception, He uses people in the process. His favorite plan is a combined effort: God plus people equals accomplishment.

I often recall the story of the preacher who saved up enough money to buy a few inexpensive acres of land. A little run-down, weather-beaten farmhouse sat on the acreage, a sad picture of years of neglect. The land had not been kept up either, so there were old tree stumps, rusted pieces of machinery, and all sorts of debris strewn here and there, not to mention a fence greatly in need of repair. The whole scene was a mess.

During his spare time and his vacations, the preacher rolled up his sleeves and got to work. He hauled off the junk, repaired the fence, pulled away the stumps, and replanted new trees. Then he refurbished the old house into a quaint cottage with a new roof, new windows, new stone walkway, new paint job, and finally a few colorful flower boxes. It took several years to accomplish all this, but finally, when the last job had been completed and he was washing up after applying a fresh coat of paint to the mailbox, his neighbor (who had watched all this from a distance) walked over and said, "Well, preacher—looks like you and the Lord have done a pretty fine job on your place here."

Wiping the sweat from his face, the minister replied, "Yeah, I suppose so . . . but you should have seen it when the Lord had it all to Himself."

God has not only created each one of us as distinct individuals, He also uses us in significant ways. Just stop and think: Chances are you are where you are today because of the words or the writings or the personal influence of certain people. I love to ask people how they became who they are. When I do, they invariably speak of the influence or the encouragement of key people in their past.

I would be the first to affirm that fact. When I look back across the landscape of my life, I am able to connect specific individuals to each crossroad and every milestone. Some of them are people the world will never know, for they are relatively unknown to the general public. But to me personally? Absolutely vital. And a few of them have remained my friends to this very day. Each one has helped me clear a hurdle or handle a struggle, accomplish an objective or endure a trial—and ultimately laugh again. I cannot even imagine where I would be today were it not for that handful of friends who have given me a heart full of joy. Let's face it, friends make life a lot more fun.

SPECIAL FRIENDS IN PAUL'S LIFE

It is easy to forget that the late, great apostle Paul needed friends too. Being ill on occasion, he needed Dr. Luke. Being limited in strength and unable to handle the rigors of extensive travel alone, he needed Barnabas and Silas. Being restricted in freedom, he needed other hands to carry his letters to their prescribed destinations. And on several occasions he needed someone to actually write out his letters. But isn't it interesting that though we know quite a bit about Paul, we know very little about his circle of friends? Yet in reality, they were part of the reason he was able to move through life as well as he did.

Returning to the letter he wrote to the Philippians, we come upon the mention of two names—a man Paul calls "my son" in another of his writings and a man he calls here "my brother." Since these two men played such significant roles in Paul's life that they deserved honorable mention, let's spend the balance of this chapter getting better acquainted with both. They were friends who made Paul's life richer and more enjoyable.

A "Son" Named Timothy

Being held under Roman guard in his house arrest, Paul found himself unable to travel back to Philippi, so he decided to send his young friend Timothy. More than any other individual, Timothy is mentioned by Paul in his writings. We saw his name earlier, in fact, in the opening line of this very letter: "Paul and Timothy, bond-servants of Christ Jesus."

Who was Timothy?

- He was a native of either Lystra or Derbe, cities in southern Asia Minor . . . today called Turkey.
- He was the child of a mixed marriage: Jewish mother (Eunice) and Greek father (never named).
- Since he remained uncircumcised until he was a young adult, Timothy's childhood upbringing was obviously more strongly influenced by the Greek than the Jewish parentage.
- However, his spiritual interest came from the maternal side of his family. Both Eunice and her mother Lois reared him to be tender toward the things of the Lord. We learn this from two comments Paul makes later in life in his second letter to his young friend.

> For I am mindful of the sincere faith within you, which first dwelt in your grandmother Lois, and your mother Eunice, and I am sure that it is in you as well.
>
> *2 Timothy 1:5*

You, however, continue in the things you have learned and become convinced of, knowing from whom you have learned them; and that from childhood you have known the sacred writings which are able to give you the wisdom that leads to salvation through faith which is in Christ Jesus.

2 Timothy 3:14–15

- Paul, no doubt, led Timothy into a personal relationship with the Lord Jesus Christ. This explains why the older referred to the younger as "my beloved and faithful child in the Lord" (1 Cor. 4:17).

- Once Timothy joined Paul (and Luke) as a traveling companion, the two remained close for the rest of Paul's life. We read of the beginning of their friendship in the early part of Acts 16.

> And he [Paul] came also to Derbe and to Lystra. And behold, a certain disciple was there, named Timothy, the son of a Jewish woman who was a believer, but his father was a Greek, and he was well spoken of by the brethren who were in Lystra and Iconium. Paul wanted this man to go with him; and he took him and circumcised him because of the Jews who were in those parts, for they all knew that his father was a Greek.

Acts 16:1–3

So much for a quick survey of Timothy's background. What is of interest to us is how Paul wrote of him to the people of Philippi.

> But I hope in the Lord Jesus to send Timothy to you shortly, so that I also may be encouraged when I learn of your condition. For I have no one else of kindred spirit who will genuinely be concerned for your welfare. For they all seek after their own interests, not those of Christ Jesus. But you know of his proven worth that he served with me in the furtherance of the gospel like a child serving his father. Therefore I hope to send him immediately, as soon as I see how things go with me; and I trust in the Lord that I myself also shall be coming shortly.

Philippians 2:19–24

As I ponder those words, three things jump out at me. All three have to do with how Paul viewed his friend.

First, *Timothy had a unique "kindred spirit" with Paul.* The single Greek term Paul used for "kindred spirit" is a combination of two words, actually: "same souled." This is the only time in all of the New Testament the term is used. We might say Paul and Timothy possessed an "equal spirit," or that they were "like-minded." Mathematically speaking, their triangles were congruent. Just think of the implications of the comment Paul makes: "I have no one else of kindred spirit."

They thought alike. Their perspectives were in line with each other. Timothy would interpret situations much like Paul, had the latter been there. In today's slang, they hit it off. When the older sent the younger on a fact-finding mission, he could rely on the report as being similar to one he himself would have brought back. Being of kindred spirit in no way suggests they had the same temperament or even that they always agreed. What it does mean, however, is that being alongside each other, neither had to work hard at the relationship; things flowed smoothly between them. I would imagine that it was not unlike the closeness David enjoyed with Jonathan, about which we read "the soul of Jonathan was knit to the soul of David, and Jonathan loved him as himself." And a little later, "he loved him as he loved his own life" (1 Sam. 18:1; 20:17).

Coming across a person with a kindred spirit is a rare find. We may have numerous casual acquaintances and several good friends in life, but finding someone who is like-souled is a most unusual (and delightful) discovery. And when it happens, both parties sense it. Neither has to convince the other that there is a oneness of spirit. It is like being with someone who lives in your own head—and vice versa—someone who reads your motives and understands your needs without either having to be stated. No need for explanations, excuses, or defenses. Paul enjoyed all these relational delights with Timothy, along with a spiritual dimension as well.

Second, *Timothy had a genuine concern for others.* That statement opens a window for us into the young man's makeup. When Timothy was with others, his heart was touched over their needs. Compassionate individuals are hard to find these days, but they were hard to find back in those days too. Remember what Paul wrote?

> For they all seek after their own interests, not those of Christ Jesus.
>
> *Philippians 2:21*

Not Timothy. Timothy modeled what Paul wrote earlier concerning an unselfish attitude.

Do nothing from selfishness or empty conceit, but with humility of mind let each of you regard one another as more important than himself; do not merely look out for your own personal interests, but also for the interests of others.

Philippians 2:3–4

That was Timothy. No wonder Paul felt so close to him. Friends like that remind us of the importance of helping others without saying a word. One man writes with understanding:

> A few years ago I stood on the banks of a river in South America and watched a young man in western clothes climb out of a primitive canoe. The veteran missionary with whom I was traveling beamed at the young man and whispered to me, "The first time I saw him he was a naked Indian kid standing right on this bank, and he pulled in my canoe for me. God gave me a real concern for him, and eventually he came to Christ, committed himself to the Lord's work and is just returning home after graduating from seminary in Costa Rica." I could understand the beam on the missionary's face, and I think Paul beamed when he talked of his men. And he had good cause to be thrilled with them.[3]

Third, *Timothy had a servant's heart.* Paul also mentioned Timothy's "proven worth," meaning "caliber"; he was that caliber of man. And what was that? He served like a child serving his father.

Question: How can one grown man serve on behalf of another grown man "like a child serving his father"?

Answer in one word: Servanthood.

In the world of leadership we are overrun with hard-charging, tough-minded, power-loving people who equate position with power. But people can wield power in any position, just as long as they maintain control over something others want.

Which reminds me of a homey little story that illustrates positional power. A new factory owner went to a nearby restaurant for a quick lunch. The menu featured a blue plate special and made it clear—absolutely no substitutions or additions. The meal was tasty, but the man needed more butter. When he asked for a second pat of butter, the waitress refused. He was so irritated he called for the manager . . . who also refused him and walked away (much to the waitress's delight). "Do you people know who I am?" he asked indignantly. "I am the owner of that factory across the street!" The waitress smiled sarcastically and whined, "Do you know who *I* am, sweetie? I'm the one who decides whether you get a second pat of butter."

Not all power moves are that blatant. Some leaders dangle others under their authority. I read a classic example of this in Leighton Ford's excellent book, *Transforming Leadership.*

Eli Black, an entrepreneurial businessman, was well-known for two things. The high point of his life was when he engineered the take-over of the United Fruit Company. The end came when he jumped from the forty-second floor of the Pan American Building in New York.

One of his executives, Thomas McCann, wrote about Black in his book *An American Company.* He describes a luncheon meeting with Black and two other managers.

As they sat down, Black smiled and asked if they were hungry. McCann replied that he was starving. Moments later a waiter came with a plate of cheese and crackers. Black reached out and took it, but instead of passing it around he placed it before him and clasped his hands in front of it.

"Now," he asked, "what's on the agenda?"

For several minutes they talked about a building they were going to put up in Costa Rica. McCann, who had not had breakfast, kept his eyes on the cheese and crackers. The only way he could get to them would be to reach across his boss's arm, and Black's body language made it clear that that would be a violation of his territory.

At a brief pause in the discussions, McCann said, "How about some cheese and crackers?" Black never even glanced at McCann, so he rephrased it. "You're not planning on eating those crackers and cheese all by yourself are you, Eli?" Again, no answer. The conversation continued, and McCann leaned back in his chair, giving up all hope of a snack.

Moments later Black made it clear that there was nothing wrong with his hearing. He continued to question and make comments.

Then, says McCann:

He unclasped his hands and picked up the knife. . . . I watched the knife dig down into the bowl of cheese; the other hand reached out and selected a Ritz cracker from the plate and Black poised the cracker on his fingertips as he carefully stroked a rounded, tantalizing mound of cheese across its face.

The cracker remained balanced on the fingertips of Black's left hand for at least the next five minutes. He asked questions about the height of the building from the street and its height above sea level . . . the color and materials . . . the size of the lobby. . . . My eyes never left the cracker. . . .

I leaned back again, this time accepting my defeat.

It was then that Black reached across the table and placed the cracker on my butter plate. He put the knife down where he had found it, and he refolded his hands before him, keeping the food within their embrace for himself alone to dispense or to keep. Black didn't say a word, but his expression made it clear that he felt he had made his point.

Eli Black symbolized perfectly one use of power. Next to truth, the power question is the most important issue for the leader. And it is precisely in relation to power that the leadership of Jesus stands in the greatest contrast to popular understandings of leadership.[4]

Unlike that entrepreneur, Timothy conformed to the Jesus model. He didn't strut his stuff. Like Paul, he served. By sending Timothy to the people of Philippi, Paul felt he was sending *himself*. No fear of offense. No anxiety over how the young man might handle some knotty problem he might encounter. Not even a passing thought that he might throw his weight around, saying, "As Paul's right-hand man. . . ." The aging apostle could rest easy. Timothy was the man for the job. Paul must have smiled when he finally waved good-bye. Friends like Timothy relieve life's pressure and enable us to smile.

A "Brother" Named Epaphroditus

Because the two men were closer, Paul wrote of who Timothy was. But when he mentions this second gentleman, Epaphroditus, he puts his finger on what he did. Another contrast: Timothy would be going to Philippi sometime in the future, but Epaphroditus would be sent immediately, probably carrying this letter Paul was writing.

Epaphroditus had been sent to Rome to minister to Paul, but shortly after arriving the man became terribly ill. Ultimately he recovered, but not before a long struggle where he lingered at death's door. News of his illness might have traveled back to Philippi, and the man was concerned that his friends back home would be worried about him. Furthermore, when he returned earlier than expected, some might think he returned as a quitter, so Paul was careful to write strong words in his defense.

But I thought it necessary to send to you Epaphroditus, my brother and fellow worker and fellow soldier, who is also your messenger and minister to my need; because he was longing for you all and was distressed because you had heard that he was sick. For indeed he was sick to the point of death, but God had mercy on him, and not on him only but also on me, lest I should have sorrow upon sorrow. Therefore I have sent him all the more eagerly in order that when you see him again you may rejoice and I may be less concerned about you. Therefore receive him in the Lord with all joy, and hold men like him in high regard; because he came close to death for the work of Christ, risking his life to complete what was deficient in your service to me.

Philippians 2:25–30

And toward the end of the same letter . . .

But I have received everything in full, and have an abundance; I am amply supplied, having received from Epaphroditus what you have sent, a fragrant aroma, an acceptable sacrifice, well-pleasing to God.

Philippians 4:18

When Epaphroditus first arrived, he brought a gift of money from the Philippians. This tells us the people back home trusted him completely. When he gave the gift to Paul, he brought enormous encouragement to the apostle . . . but shortly thereafter, Epaphroditus fell ill. So the apostle writes with deep affection, referring to him as, "brother . . . fellow worker . . . fellow soldier . . . messenger . . . minister to my need." I'd call those admirable qualities in a friend. Bishop Lightfoot says that Epaphroditus was one in "common sympathy, common work, and common danger and toil and suffering"[5] with the great apostle. When you've got someone near you with credentials like that, life doesn't seem nearly as heavy.

- Why did Paul send Epaphroditus back? To put the people at ease and to cause them to rejoice (there's that word again) upon hearing from Paul by letter.
- What was to be their response back home? Extend a joyful welcome and hold Epaphroditus in high regard.
- Why did he deserve their respect? Because he had risked his life in coming to minister to Paul . . . he had exposed

himself to danger. We would say he had flirted with death to be near his friend.

In those days when people visited prisoners who were held captive under Roman authority, they were often prejudged as criminal types as well. Therefore, a visitor exposed himself to danger just by being near those who were considered dangerous. The Greek term Paul uses here for "risking"—*paraboleuomai*—is one that meant "to hazard with one's life . . . to gamble." Epaproditus did just that.

In the early church there were societies of men and women who called themselves *the parabolani,* that is, *the riskers or gamblers.* They ministered to the sick and imprisoned, and they saw to it that, if at all possible, martyrs and sometimes even enemies would receive an honorable burial. Thus in the city of Carthage during the great pestilence of A.D. 252 Cyprian, the bishop, showed remarkable courage. In self-sacrificing fidelity to his flock, and love even for his enemies, he took upon himself the care of the sick, and bade his congregation nurse them and bury the dead. What a contrast with the practice of the heathen who were throwing the corpses out of the plague-stricken city and were running away in terror![6]

A special joy binds two friends who are not reluctant to risk danger on each other's behalf. If a true friend finds you're in need, he or she will find a way to help. Nor will a friend ever ask, "How great is the risk?" The question is always, "When do you need me?" Not even the threat of death holds back a friend.

This reminds me of the six-year-old girl who became deathly ill with a dread disease. To survive, she needed a blood transfusion from someone who had previously conquered the same illness. The situation was complicated by her rare blood type. Her nine-year-old brother qualified as a donor, but everyone was hesitant to ask him since he was just a lad. Finally they agreed to have the doctor pose the question.

The attending physician tactfully asked the boy if he was willing to be brave and donate blood for his sister. Though he didn't understand much about such things, the boy agreed without hesitation: "Sure, I'll give my blood for my sister."

He lay down beside his sister and smiled at her as they pricked his arm with the needle. Then he closed his eyes and lay silently on the bed as the pint of blood was taken.

Soon thereafter the physician came in to thank the little fellow. The boy, with quivering lips and tears running down his cheeks, asked, "Doctor, when do I die?" At that moment the doctor realized that the naive little boy thought that by giving his blood, he was giving up his life. Quickly he reassured the lad that he was not going to die, but amazed at his courage, the doctor asked, "Why were you willing to risk your life for her?"

"Because she is my sister . . . and I love her," was the boy's simple but significant reply.

So it was between Epaphroditus and his brother in Rome . . . and so it is to this day. Danger and risk don't threaten true friendship; they strengthen it. Such friends are modern-day members of *the parabolani*, that reckless band of friends—riskers and gamblers, all—who love their brothers and sisters to the uttermost. Each one deserves our respect. When we need them, they are there. I have a few in that category. Hopefully, you do too.

THREE PEOPLE WHO DESERVE A RESPONSE

As I think about how all this ties in with our lives today, I am reminded of three categories of special people and how we are to respond to them.

First, there are still a few Timothys left on earth, thank goodness. *When God sends a Timothy into our lives, He expects us to relate to him.* It is often the beginning of an intimate friendship, rarely experienced in our day of superficial companionship. With a Timothy, you won't have to force a friendship; it will flow. Nor will you find yourself dreading the relationship; it will be rewarding. When a Timothy comes along, don't hesitate . . . *relate.*

Second, there may be a modern-day Epaphroditus who comes to your assistance or your rescue. *When God sends an Epaphroditus to minister to us, He expects us to respect him.* This is the type of person who reaches out when he has nothing to gain and perhaps much to lose . . . who gambles on your behalf for no other reason than love. His or her action is an act of grace. Don't question it or try to repay it or make attempts to bargain for it. Just accept it. Grace extended in love is to be accepted with gratitude. The best response to an Epaphroditus? *Respect.*

And there is a third person I haven't said much about in a personal way. But since we are approximately halfway through Paul's letter, as well as this book, it is time I introduced you to this third friend. His name is Jesus Christ. *Since God sent Christ to take away our sins and bring us to heaven, He expects us to receive Him.* If you think a Timothy can mean a lot to you or an Epaphroditus could prove invaluable, let me assure you that neither can compare as a substitute for Jesus. With nail-scarred hands He reaches out to you and waits for you to reach back in faith. I tell you without a moment's hesitation, there is no one you will ever meet, no friend you will ever make, who can do for you what Jesus can do. No one else can change your inner heart. No one else can turn your entire life around. No one else can remove not only your sins but the guilt and shame that are part of that whole ugly package. And now that the two of you have been introduced, only one response is appropriate. Only one. *Receive.*

I began this chapter by stating that people need other people. You need me. I need you. Both of us need a few kindred spirits, people who understand us and encourage us. Both of us need friends who are willing to risk to help us and, yes, at times, to rescue us. Friends like that make life more fun. But all of us—you, me, Timothy-people, Epaphroditus-people, *all of us*—need a Savior. He awaits your response. The everlasting relief He brings is enough to make us not only laugh again, but laugh forever.

8

Happy Hopes for High Achievers

*L*AST NIGHT I MET A MAN who told me he needed to work harder at being happier.

He said he had been reared in an ultraserious home. "We didn't talk about our feelings . . . *we worked*. My father, my mother, most of my sisters and brothers bought into that way of life," he sighed. "Somehow we all had the idea that you could achieve whatever you wanted in life if you just worked hard enough and long enough." And then he came to the crux of his concern: "Funny thing . . . in my sixty-plus years I have achieved about everything I dreamed of doing and I have been awarded for it. My problem is that I don't know how to have fun and enjoy all these things hard work has brought me. I cannot remember the last time I laughed—I mean *really* laughed."

As he turned to walk away, I thought this throwaway line was the most revealing thing he said: "I suppose I now need to work harder at being happier."

I reached over, took him by the arm, and pulled him back close enough to put my arms around him for a solid, manly hug. "You've worked hard for everything else in your life," I said quietly. "Why not try a new approach for joy? Trust me on this one—a happy heart is not achieved by hard work and long hours. If it were, the happiest people on earth would be the workaholics . . . and I have never met a workaholic whose sense of humor balanced out his intensity." We talked a few more minutes, but I'm not sure I made a dent in his thinking. Most likely, at this very moment that high achiever is up and at it (it's early Monday morning) pursuing a game plan to earn happiness. *It ain't gonna happen.*

The problem is that human achievement results in earthly rewards, which fuels the fire for more achievement leading to greater rewards.

"Problem . . . what problem?" you and the man I met last night may ask. This: None of that results in deep-down satisfaction, an inner peace, a soul-level contentment, or lasting joy. In the process of achieving more and earning more, few if any learn to laugh more. This is especially true if you're the classic Type A. Hear me out.

Something within all of us warms up to human strokes. We are motivated to do more when our efforts are noticed and rewarded. That is why they make things like impressive trophies and silver platters and bronze plaques and gold medals. Most folks love putting those things on display. Whether it is an athletic letter on a sweater in high school or a Salesperson-of-the-Month plaque on the wall, we like the recognition. What does it do? It drives us on to do more, to gain greater recognition, to achieve more valuable rewards, better pay, or higher promotions.

Virtually every major field of endeavor has its particular award for outstanding achievement. Universities award scholarships; companies give bonuses; the film industry offers the Oscar; the television industry, the Emmy; the music industry, the Grammy; and the writing industry, the Pulitzer Prize. The athletic world has an entire spectrum of honors. Whether garnering individual awards for exceptional achievement or team trophies for championship play, winning players are applauded and record-setting coaches are affirmed (and envied). Furthermore, most folks are awed simply by being around celebrities. Recently I read a funny story that perfectly illustrates this fact:

> A tourist was standing in line to buy an ice cream cone at a Thrifty Drug store in Beverly Hills. To her utter shock and amazement, who should walk in and stand right behind her but Paul Newman! Well the lady, even though she was rattled, determined to maintain her composure. She purchased her ice cream cone and turned confidently and exited the store.
>
> However, to her horror, she realized that she had left the counter without her ice cream cone! She waited a few minutes till she felt all was clear, and then went back into the store to claim her cone. As she approached the counter, the cone was not in the little circular receptacle, and for a moment she stood there pondering what might have happened to it. The she felt a polite tap on her shoulder, and turning was confronted by—you guessed it—Paul Newman. The famous actor then told the lady that if she was looking for her ice cream cone, she had put it into her purse![1]

While I was sitting in the Great Western Forum the other evening watching the Los Angeles Lakers, I looked up toward the ceiling and saw all those NBA championship banners hanging high. I glanced toward one wall bright with spotlights and read the names on jerseys that have been retired: Baylor, Chamberlain, West, Abdul-Jabbar, and, most recently, Johnson. What an honor to have one's name placed on public display for all the world to see! It is society's way of saying, "You are great!"

There is nothing wrong with that as long as we remember it is an earthly system exalting earthly people who are rewarded for earthly accomplishments. But how easy it is to forget that not one of those accomplishments gives a person what he or she may lack deep within—that's why they can't bring lasting satisfaction. And much more importantly, none of them earns God's favor.

THE GREAT TEMPTATION AMONG HIGH ACHIEVERS

All this leads me to a terribly important subject I have been wanting to address. Having had that conversation with Mr. High Achiever last evening, I'm unable to restrain myself any longer . . . and I especially have in mind those of you who can't stand coming in second because you face a great temptation.

What is it? It is the temptation to believe that earthly honors will automatically result in heavenly rewards. This kind of thinking is at the root of a humanistic philosophy of life that says: "By working hard and accomplishing more than most, I will earn God's favor and receive His nod of approval." I don't know of a more subtle, albeit heretical, philosophy than that, yet it is universally accepted as true. And so, the tragedy is, enough is never enough. Life is reduced to work, tasks, effort, an endless list of shoulds and musts . . . minus the necessary fun and laughter that keeps everything in perspective.

Why does it happen? What is it that drives us on so relentlessly? Are you ready? Take a deep breath and allow yourself to tolerate the one-word answer: PRIDE. We work and push and strive so we can prove we are worthy . . . we are the best . . . we deserve top honors. And the hidden message: I can gain righteousness all on my own, by my own effort, ingenuity, and energy. And because I can, I must! And why is this heretical? Because ultimately this philosophy says: (1) I really won't need divine righteousness (after all, God helps those who help themselves, right?), and (2) I will find lasting joy in my own achievement. This will

127

bring me ultimate satisfaction. Both are dead-end roads found on Fantasy Island.

A longtime friend of mine openly confessed:

> Work had always been highly esteemed in our family, and hard work was seen as the primary tool for success. I figured if it were good to work ten hours, it would be even better to work fourteen.
>
> In college, I seemed to have the energy to withstand the pressure. I remember times at Stanford when I wouldn't even go home at night. Instead, I would push a table up near the door of the cafeteria at 3 a.m. and sleep on it, using my books as a pillow. And then in the morning, when I had to be at work, the first person to open the door would knock me off the table, and I'd wake up and start the day. I convinced myself that I was sleeping "faster" than anyone else. . . .
>
> During the years when I was a coach and an area director for Young Life, I would work twelve, fourteen, even fifteen hours a day, six or seven days a week. And I would come home feeling that I hadn't worked enough. So I tried to cram even more into my schedule. I spent more time promoting living than I did living. . . . My life wasn't abundant; it was a frantic sprint from one hour to the next.
>
> I can remember times when fatigue left me feeling isolated and alienated—feelings that previously had been foreigners to me. Unprepared for such parasites on my energy, I became frustrated, and laughter, which had always been my most treasured companion, had silently slipped away. . . .
>
> I was dominated by "shoulds," and "ought to's," and "musts." I would awaken unrefreshed in the morning, with a tired kind of resentment, and hurry through the day trying to uncover and meet the demands of others. Days were not lived but endured. I was exhausted trying to be a hope constantly rekindled for others, straining to live up to their images of me. I had worked hard to develop a reputation as one who was concerned, available, and involved—now I was being tyrannized by it. Often I was more at peace in the eyes of others than in my own.
>
> The Western mind and culture leave little time for leisure, prayer, play, and contemplation. Hurry needs answers; answers need categories; categories need labeling and dissecting. The pace I was trying to maintain had no time for rhythm and awe, for mystery and wonder. I barely had time to care adequately for friends or for myself. In order to keep up my incessant activity, God was simply reduced to fit into my schedule. I suffered, because he didn't fit.[2]

Pride not only expresses itself in high-achieving hard work, but also keeps us from asking for help. We love to leave the impression that no matter what, we can handle it—no help wanted!

I remember when my family and I lived in New England. We weren't accustomed to snow in the winter. It threw us a real nasty curve. We found ourselves somewhat confused when we faced our first wintry blast. For example, I couldn't figure out why people didn't park on the street. I thought, *That's the best place in the world . . . nobody parks there. In fact, there are no "No Parking" signs anywhere.* So I parked on the street. I remember being sort of proud of my original idea when I locked the car for the night. That was about the time the snow began to fall. In fact, it snowed all night. It never even dawned on me that snowplows worked the street all night long, pushing back the fallen snow.

The next morning when I crawled out of our warm bed, I discovered why nobody parked on the street. I looked out front and thought somebody had stolen my car! Stunned to find huge mounds of crusted snow and ice on both sides of the street, I took my pick and shovel and began to do archaeological work in hopes of finding a blue four-door sedan. After digging like mad for at least twenty minutes, I finally got to something hard. When I saw blue I thought, *That's my color . . . must be my car.* About that time a friend drove by. He stopped, smiled, rolled down his window, and asked, "Hey, Chuck, can I help you?" I immediately responded, "No, thanks—I'm doing fine." He shrugged and drove on. About half an hour later I wondered why I hadn't said yes. The simple answer: I was proud. I could dig out my own car, thank you. Stupid pride!

You know what else I did? When I finally got down to my ice-covered car and saw all the ice on the windows, my first thought was, *It's dumb to stand here and scrape off all that ice.* So I went inside and got a bucket of steaming hot water and dumped it over the front window. Trust me, not only did the ice come off, so did my windshield. I was stunned as it shattered with a loud bang and fell into the front seat. I thought, *So that's why everybody scrapes the ice off windshields.* Let me tell you, when I drove the car to the glass shop, I had clear vision! It was ten degrees in the car, but I had clear vision.

Do you know the first thing I did when I broke my front window? I looked around to see if anybody was watching. Why? Pride, plain and simple. I didn't want anyone to know what a foolish thing I had done. Pride encourages us to hide our stupidity rather than admit it. And I remember that throughout the entire episode I did not have much fun. I don't recall laughing either at myself or at my circumstance.

There is always that one telltale sign when pride takes charge: the fun leaves. A driven high achiever may smile on occasion, but it is a surface grin, not a strong, quiet sense of satisfaction. Deep within, he or she is really thinking, *Life is much too busy, much too serious to waste it on silly things like relaxation and laughter.* Staying wound up that tight can cause the mind to snap. G. K. Chesterton was never more correct than when he wrote, "Madmen are always serious; they go mad from lack of humour."[3]

THE HONEST TESTIMONY OF A HIGH-ACHIEVING PHARISEE

All this brings us back to a little letter written to a small band of believers living in ancient Philippi. Because the writer, Paul, felt so close to them, he wasn't afraid to be honest and allow them to see the dark side of his past. But before doing so he underscores the underlying theme of his letter by reminding them to find the joy in living.

> Finally, my brethren, rejoice in the Lord. To write the same things again is no trouble to me, and it is a safeguard for you.
>
> *Philippians 3:1*

The Living Bible says:

> Whatever happens, dear friends, be glad in the Lord. I never get tired of telling you this and it is good for you to hear it again and again.

Paul is about to launch into his past—those intense years of his own existence when he worked so hard to impress God. But before he does that, he wants to make sure that they hear yet again the importance of being people of outrageous joy. He calls that "a safeguard." How true. Not only were the pressures of life enough to steal their joy, there were also the ever-present legalists—ancient grace killers—on the loose. And nobody can rob people of joy quicker than a few narrow-minded legalists. Paul's great concern was that his Philippian friends continue to enjoy their freedom in Christ and not allow *anything* or *anyone* to get the best of them. He never got tired of telling them that.

A Warning to His Close Friends

I am not dreaming up the idea that legalists were on the loose. Neither have I been too strong in my comments. Paul himself calls them "dogs . . . evil workers." See for yourself:

> Beware of the dogs, beware of the evil workers, beware of the false circumcision.
>
> *Philippians 3:2*

Strong words! When he refers to them as dogs, Paul doesn't have in mind the little lap dogs we enjoy as pets or those obedient, loyal creatures we pamper and nourish. No, the dogs of his day were dirty, disease-carrying scavengers who ran in packs through the streets and narrow alleys of a city. Unable to be controlled and potentially dangerous, they posed a menacing threat to anyone who got in their way. With that word picture in mind, Paul warns, "Watch out . . . beware! These people will assault you and you will lose your joy."

He goes further: "Beware of evil workers." These legalists taught that people were saved by works—by keeping the Law (an impossibility). Such folks live on to this day, spreading their heresy. Their message is full of exhortations to do more, to work harder, to witness longer, to pray with greater intensity, because enough is never enough. Such folks are "evil workers" who will take away what little bit of joy you may be able to muster. I would also add that when you never know how much is enough to satisfy God, you are left in a continual state of shame and obligation. Your mind never rests. The message of the legalists always finds you lacking. It never brings relief. We need to beware of such messengers. They are, according to Scripture, evil workers.

By calling them "false circumcision" people, Paul meant they believed in mutilation, not merely circumcision, for salvation. They taught, if circumcision was good, castration was even better! One *must* (there's that word again) work exceptionally hard to be acceptable to God—give up, take on, put away, add to, try harder, contribute more—before there could be assurance of divine acceptance. The result of all that? Confidence in the flesh! You worked hard . . . you sacrificed . . . you labored intensely . . . you received it. And in the process you had every reason to be proud of it. I say again . . . heresy!

With quiet and firm reassurance, Paul communicates the simple truth to his friends:

> For we are the true circumcision, who worship in the Spirit of God and glory in Christ Jesus and put no confidence in the flesh.
>
> *Philippians 3:3*

Those last six words—"put no confidence in the flesh"—what a helpful relief! God's grace has again come to our rescue. And in the process He gets the glory. All the credit goes to Him, as certainly it should. When it comes to our vertical and eternal relationship with God, unlike the humanist's message, we put no confidence in the flesh. Salvation through human works? No way. Human pride? No reason. The gift that brings back the laughter—God's gift of eternal life with Him—is based on what He has done for us and not what we have done for Him. Maybe you need to read that sentence again. It explains why we put no confidence in the flesh. Those who do have missed the whole point of grace.

A Revealing of His Proud Record

These words about "confidence in the flesh" triggered a lot of emotion in Paul. While writing them he must have experienced a flashback to the way he was for so many years—in fact, all of his adult life. Before his conversion, he was the personification of a proud Pharisee. Nobody's trophy case was larger. Had they given an award for high achievement in the field of religion, Paul would have won top honors in his nation year after year after year. His wall could have been covered with plaques, diplomas, framed letters from influential individuals, and numerous artifacts—all impressive.

> . . . If anyone else has a mind to put confidence in the flesh, I far more.
>
> *Philippians 3:4*

When he writes those words, Paul is not padding the report or trying to appear important. As we are about to read, he had earned the respect of every law-keeping Judaizer in the known world. When he said, "I far more," he had the record to prove it. For example:

Circumcised the eighth day, of the nation of Israel, of the tribe of Benjamin, a Hebrew of Hebrews; as to the Law, a Pharisee; as to zeal, a persecutor of the church; as to the righteousness which is in the Law, found blameless.

Philippians 3:5–6

That pedigree and brief list of achievements may not seem impressive to you today, especially if you are not Jewish, but do not discount their significance. Paul was the ultimate high achiever of his day. As one New Testament scholar explains:

If ever there was a Jew who was steeped in Judaism, that Jew was Paul. Let us . . . look again at the claims he had to be the Jew *par excellence*. . . . He was circumcised on the eighth day; that is to say, he bore in the body the badge and the mark that he was one of the chosen people, marked out by God as His own. He was of the race of Israel; that is to say, he was a member of the nation who stood in a covenant relationship with God, a relationship in which no other people stood. He was of the tribe of Benjamin. This is a claim which Paul reiterates in *Romans* 11:1. What is the point of this claim? The tribe of Benjamin had a unique place in the history of Israel. It was from Benjamin that the first king of Israel had come, for Saul was a Benjamite . . . . Benjamin was the only one of the patriarchs who had actually been born in the land of promise. When Israel went into battle, it was the tribe of Benjamin which held the post of honour. The battle-cry of Israel was: "After thee, O Benjamin". . . .

In lineage Paul was not only an Israelite; he was of the aristocracy of Israel. He was a Hebrew of the Hebrews; that is to say, Paul was not one of these Jews of the Dispersion who, in a foreign land, had forgotten their own tongue; he was a Jew who still remembered and knew the language of his fathers.

He was a Pharisee; that is to say, he was not only a devout Jew; he was more—he was one of "The Separated Ones" who had foresworn all normal activities in order to dedicate life to the keeping of the Law, and he had kept it with such meticulous care that in the keeping of it he was blameless.

. . . Paul knew Judaism at its best and at its highest; he knew it from the inside; he had gone through all the experiences, both of height and of depth, that it could bring to any man.[4]

Did you observe how Paul categorized his achievements? On an accelerated scale:

- "As to the Law"
- "As to zeal"
- "As to righteousness"

It is the last one that stands out—the ultimate! "When I added up all those things in my mind, I had arrived. When compared to all others, I qualified as *righteous*." Paul outstripped all his contemporaries, eclipsed all other lights. As A. T. Robertson summed up so eloquently, Paul had—

> A marvellous record, scoring a hundred in Judaism.
> . . . He was the star of hope for Gamaliel and the Sanhedrin.[5]

In today's terms, that proud Pharisee known as Saul of Tarsus won all the marbles—the Pulitzer, the Medal of Honor, the Most Valuable Player, the Heisman, the Gold Medal . . . the Nobel of Ancient Jewry. Had they had newspapers or magazines in his day, his picture would have been on the front page, and the headlines would have read, RELIGIOUS ZEALOT OF THE DECADE. His was the name dropped by everybody who was anybody. Any search for a model to follow would have led to the scholar from Tarsus, but you would have to move fast to stay up. He wasn't nearly finished with his plan to rid the world of Christians. The last entry in his Daytimer read, "Next stop: Damascus." On that fateful trip, everything changed.

A Change in His Entire Life

While riding the crest of that wave of international fame, Saul of Tarsus met his match in the person of Jesus Christ. While still on the outskirts of the city of Damascus, he was suddenly struck blind by a blazing light from heaven and silenced by a voice that must have sounded like the roar of a dozen Niagaras: "Saul . . . Saul . . . why are you persecuting Me?" Though blinded by the light, at that moment the Pharisee got his first glimpse of perfect righteousness. And for the first time in his life he was humbled. His robes of self-righteousness were nothing more than filthy rags. All his trophies and plaques and impressive earthly honors were as worthless as wood, hay, and stubble. One glimpse of true, heaven-sent righteousness was enough to convince him forever that he had spent his entire life on the wrong road traveling at breakneck speed toward the wrong destination for all the wrong reasons.

Now we can appreciate the importance of that little word "but" in the midst of Paul's listing of all his achievements:

> But whatever things were gain to me, those things I have counted as loss for the sake of Christ. More than that, I count all things to be loss in view of the surpassing value of knowing Christ Jesus my Lord, for whom I have suffered the loss of all things, and count them but rubbish in order that I may gain Christ, and may be found in Him, not having a righteousness of my own derived from the Law, but that which is through faith in Christ, the righteousness which comes from God on the basis of faith.
>
> *Philippians 3:7–9*

But! God called an abrupt and absolute halt to Saul's maddening pace. His entire frame of reference was altered. His whole perspective changed. His way of thinking and, of course, his way of life were radically transformed from that day forward. He saw, for the first time, how utterly and completely misguided he had been. As this newfound, divine perspective replaced the old hunger for earthly applause and the old drive for human righteousness, he felt himself bankrupt, reduced to ground zero. And all those honors he had worked for and relished for so long? He counted them as "loss" and "rubbish." Having clothed himself in the pride of self-achievement, he now stood stark naked and spiritually bankrupt. Having once set records when evaluated by other men and women, he now realized what a total failure he had been when appraised by his Master and Lord. And at that epochal moment divine righteousness was credited to his empty account, and he saw himself reclothed in the imputed righteousness of Christ. That changed everything within him and about him.

A Statement of His Consuming Passion

Did all of life stop there? Was that all there was to it? Hardly. That was when Paul really started to live. It was at that point the man began to laugh again! With a transformed heart he testified that his desire regarding Christ was that he might—

> . . . know Him, and the power of His resurrection and the fellowship of

His sufferings, being conformed to His death; in order that I may attain to the resurrection from the dead.

Philippians 3:10–11

It is difficult to believe that a man as hard-charging and determined as Saul of Tarsus could pen such tender words. Look at them again. Perhaps we could call them Paul's credo. Rather than being driven by confidence in the flesh, his consuming passion was to spend the balance of his years on earth knowing Christ more intimately, drawing upon His resurrection power more increasingly, entering into His sufferings more personally, and being conformed to His image more completely. His dreams of making it all on his own were forever dashed on the solid rock of Jesus Christ.

THE PLAIN TRUTH TO ALL WHO RESPOND

If you are among the high achievers I've been writing to in this chapter, I commend you for reading this far. These are not the kinds of things you normally think about, I realize. Your world doesn't leave much room for personal weakness, does it? You don't rely on help from anything (or anyone) but your own reservoir of resourcefulness, do you? All your life you've been coming on strong, fighting and pushing for top honors and hopefully getting your own sweet way, haven't you? The things you are most proud of are your achievements, naturally, for that's really all you've got to show for all your hard work. In many ways, you've arrived, at least in the opinion of others. Yours is an enviable list of accomplishments. Let me name a few:

- Your respected position with a nice-sounding title
- Your salary with some enviable perks
- Your growing popularity among your peers
- Those awards you've hung on your walls
- That fine automobile sitting in your parking space (and that parking space!)
- A wardrobe full of elegant and stylish clothes
- A nice place to go home to . . . maybe more than a summer home . . . a winter home

- The probability of accomplishing and earning more
- A sense of power in knowing you can buy whatever you want any time you want it
- The feeling of accomplishment—you did it!

Granted, those are the kinds of things most folks you know spend their entire lives hoping to achieve. And now you find yourself a member of that elite club: High Achievers Anonymous (except by then they're not usually anonymous). Maybe we could say they are members of the MITTT Club—*Made It to the Top.*

But let's look deeper. Let's look at another list:

- How is your personal life? I'm referring to the real you that's there when nobody's looking . . . like when you're all alone in your car or boat or plane. Are you personally contented and at peace?
- And what about your marriage? And your relationship with your children? Everything okay there?
- While you are allowing me to get this close, may we take a look at your inner person? Are you secure or still rather afraid? Any habits out of control? Any addictions you can't seem to conquer?
- Let me ask a few what ifs: What if you became ill? What if you lost your earning power? What if you lost your title? What if your next physical exam led to the discovery of a lump . . . and that lump proved malignant? What if you had a stroke? Are you ready to die?
- Are there some secrets that haunt you? Are there some terrorizing worries that won't go away . . . that money won't erase?
- Finally, has life become more fun for you? Do you laugh—I mean really laugh—now that you have "arrived"? Or are you still too driven to relax?

If you've answered those questions honestly—or even taken the time to read them—then you're ready to hear the rest.

First, spending your life trusting in your own achievements brings you the glory now but leaves you spiritually bankrupt forever. Read that again, please. And as you do, think of that first-century man we've been reading about, Saul of Tarsus. Think of what his life would have been if he had never responded positively to the claims of Christ.

Second, stopping today and trusting in Christ's accomplishment on the cross will give Him the glory now and provide you with perfect righteousness forever.

You're intelligent, so let me ask you: *Which option makes better sense?* And just in case you think high achievers can't change, remember that man from Tarsus. He didn't merely exchange one religion for another . . . he didn't swap off one system of rites and ceremonies for another system of rules and regulations. The popular opinion these days is that folks need to change their religion or start going to a different church. That is nonsense. Saul didn't get a new religion or merely change churches after his Damascus Road experience. He was thoroughly and radically converted, like the man who wrote these words:

> I had walked life's path with an easy tread,
> Had followed where comfort and pleasure led;
> And then by chance in a quiet place—
> I met my Master face to face.
>
> With station and rank and wealth for goal,
> Much thought for body but none for soul,
> I had entered to win this life's mad race—
> When I met my Master face to face.
>
> I had built my castles, reared them high,
> Till their towers had pierced the blue of the sky;
> I had sworn to rule with an iron mace—
> When I met my Master face to face.
>
> I met Him and knew Him, and blushed to see
> That His eyes full of sorrow were fixed on me;
> And I faltered, and fell at His feet that day
> While my castles vanished and melted away.
>
> Melted and vanished; and in their place
> I saw naught else but my Master's face;
> And I cried aloud: "Oh, make me meet
> To follow the marks of Thy wounded feet."

My thought is now for the souls of men;
I have lost my life to find it again
Ever since alone in that holy place
My master and I stood face to face.[6]

9

Hanging Tough Together . . . and Loving It

ONE DAY EVERY YEAR LITTLE BOYS all across America dream big dreams. They may not say so, but inside their heads are mental images of themselves being viewed by millions of people all around the world. In their imaginations they will one day wear the uniform and be a part of some championship team battling for the ultimate prize, a sparkling silver trophy in the shape of a football. We call that day of dreams "Super Bowl Sunday." Amazingly, a few of those little boys who dream big dreams do wind up playing in the big game.

Over twenty-five years ago when the first Super Bowl game was played, a ten-year-old boy sat beside his father in the stands of the Los Angeles Coliseum. As he watched players like Bart Starr, Paul Hornung, Boyd Dowler, Fuzzy Thurston, Carrol Dale, and other outstanding athletes on Vince Lombardi's great Green Bay Packers team dominate their opponents, he daydreamed of one day being down on that gridiron. And that is exactly what happened as James Lofton, a wide receiver for the Buffalo Bills (and the oldest man on the team), finally made it to the top and had his dream come true. Through strong and weak seasons, team changes, and several injuries as a professional football player, Lofton persevered—and his determination paid off. The Bills haven't won a Super Bowl, but James Lofton played in two of them.[1]

I cannot tell you what makes football fans out of other people, but I can tell you why I follow the game with such interest. Far beyond the smashing and the pounding, the aches and pains of the game, I see an analogy between football and life. Those who hang tough, refusing to give up no matter how difficult or demanding or disappointing the challenges may be, are the ones who stand the best chance of winning. They are also the ones who find the greatest satisfaction and delight in their years on earth. Henry David Thoreau said it best:

If one advances confidently in the direction of his dreams, and endeavors to live the life which he has imagined, he will meet with a success unexpected in common hours.[2]

That may sound like the ending to a fairy tale, almost as if some Disney character were telling us to wish upon a star while standing near the castle in Fantasyland, but it is not that at all. I see in Thoreau's statement a long and untiring determination in the same direction. Not a get-rich-quick scheme or some overnight success plan, but a confident advancement in the right direction over the long haul. Dreams are important, no question; yet they must be mixed with the patient discipline of staying at the tough tasks, regardless.

A BRIEF STOP AT TODAY'S BOOKSHELVES

This is not the popular message we hear today. I was struck by this realization recently while browsing through a new bookstore not far from my home. As I wandered through the section on management and motivation, the titles made a bold statement about how society feels regarding patience and long-term diligence:

- *Passport to Prosperity*
- *Winning Moves*
- *True Greed*
- *Leadership Secrets of Attila the Hun*
- *Winning Through Intimidation*
- *Cashing In on the American Dream (How to Retire at 35)*
- *The Art of Selfishness*
- *Techniques That Take You to the Top*
- *How to Get What You Really Want*
- *Secrets to Quick Success*

Who's kidding whom? In spite of all those eye-catching, cleverly worded titles, the so-called secret to quick *anything* beneficial is light-years removed from the truth. In the final analysis, the race is won by right objectives relentlessly pursued. Whether it is an athlete reaching the Super Bowl, parents rearing a houseful of kids, a young woman earning her Ph.D., or a gifted musician perfecting his skill on an instrument, hanging tough over the long haul is still the investment that pays the richest dividends. And, I might add, it brings the greatest joy.

A Lingering Look at Paul's Prescription

In the previous chapter we looked at the former life of the apostle Paul. As a young scholar he had won bragging rights over all his peers. His heritage, his schooling, his accomplishments, his zeal, his position, his passion were all part of his being groomed for a seat on the Supreme Court of the Jews, the Sanhedrin. That all-powerful name recognition gave him the edge . . . until he was intercepted by the resurrected, sovereign Christ . . . stunned and crushed by the revelation of the Son of God.

John Pollock, in a work entitled *The Man Who Shook the World,* describes it well.

> Paul could not believe what he heard and saw. All his convictions, intellect and training, his reputation, his self respect, demanded that Jesus should not be alive again. He played for time and replied, "Who are you, Lord?" He used a mode of address which might mean no more than "Your honor."
>
> "I am Jesus, whom you are persecuting. It is hard for you, this kicking against the goad."
>
> Then he knew. In a second that seemed an eternity Paul saw the wounds in Jesus' hands and feet, saw the face and knew that he had seen the Lord, that he was alive, as Stephen and the others had said, and that he loved not only those whom Paul persecuted but Paul: "It is hard for *you* to kick against the goad." Not one word of reproach.
>
> Paul had never admitted to himself that he had felt pricks of a goad as he raged against Stephen and his disciples. But now, instantaneously, he was shatteringly aware that he had been fighting Jesus. And fighting himself, his conscience, his powerlessness, the darkness and chaos in his soul. God hovered over this chaos and brought him to the moment of new creation. It wanted only his "Yes."
>
> Paul broke.
>
> He was trembling and in no state to weigh the pros and cons of changing sides. He only knew that he had heard a voice and had seen the Lord, and that nothing mattered but to find and obey his will.
>
> "What shall I do, Lord?"[3]

I was sitting in chapel back in 1959 at Dallas Theological Seminary, listening to Dr. Alan Redpath, then pastor of the famed Moody Memorial Church. I was taking notes, as I often did while listening to chapel speakers, and suddenly I stopped writing. Dr. Redpath had made a statement that burned its way deeply into the creases of my brain: "When God wants to do an impossible task, He takes an impossible man and crushes him." In the intervening years I have learned how right Dr. Redpath was. That is often the plan God uses when dealing with strong-willed, stubborn people.

Paul was both, so we should not be surprised that he was crushed. "Shattered," says Pollack. That is why verse 7 of Philippians 3 begins with "but." In effect, Paul admits, "I had achieved all those honors, I had won all the awards, I had gotten all the applause, I had impressed all my contemporaries . . . *but* God pulled every one of them off the wall. He put all that into correct perspective as He crushed my pride, won my heart, and came to live within me."

> But whatever things were gain to me, those things I have counted as loss for the sake of Christ. More than that, I count all things to be loss in view of the surpassing value of knowing Christ Jesus my Lord, for whom I have suffered the loss of all things, and count them but rubbish in order that I may gain Christ, and may be found in Him, not having a righteousness of my own derived from the Law, but that which is through faith in Christ, the righteousness which comes from God on the basis of faith.
>
> *Philippians 3:7–9*

I have been justified! God's love has invaded! Christ's presence has taken up residence! He has changed me! The load of sin is lifted . . . the source of righteousness has shifted! My relationship with God now rests on faith, not works. What a relief!

Paul was clearly a changed man. To his own amazement he began to laugh again.

But what now? Had he arrived? Was there nothing more to do but sit around and dream, dream, dream? No. In his own words, "I press on . . . I press on."

> Not that I have already obtained it, or have already become perfect, but I press on in order that I may lay hold of that for which also I was laid

hold of by Christ Jesus. Brethren, I do not regard myself as having laid hold of it yet; but one thing I do: forgetting what lies behind and reaching forward to what lies ahead, I press on toward the goal for the prize of the upward call of God in Christ Jesus. Let us therefore, as many as are perfect, have this attitude; and if in anything you have a different attitude, God will reveal that also to you; however, let us keep living by that same standard to which we have attained.

Philippians 3:12–16

I find his opening lines not a little relieving. With a background like his it would be easy to think he had life by the tail. I've met a few superpious men and women who held a rather inflated opinion of themselves, almost to the point where you wonder if they have started to believe all their own press releases. (I confess, when I come across people like that, I have this strong urge to visit with their married partners and ask them what it is like living with someone who has "arrived." Mates are good at setting the record straight.)

As I read over Paul's comments, which sort of summarize his philosophy of life, five ideas emerge.

1. The plan is progress, not perfection. Twice, right out of the chute, he states that he is far from perfect: "Not that I have obtained it . . . become perfect . . . I do not regard myself as having laid hold of it yet. . . ."

What is "it"? Christlikeness. True and complete godliness in final form, with no room for improvement. Nobody on earth qualifies for this one.

Part of the reason hanging tough is tough is the imperfection that continues to mark our lives. Frequent reminders of our humanity still rear their ugly heads. That is true of ourselves, and it is true of others. We, ourselves, are imperfect, living in an imperfect world, surrounded by imperfect people, who continue to model imperfections on a daily basis. Happy is the person who keeps that in mind. You will find that life is not nearly as galling if you remember that the goal is to press on in spite of the lack of perfection.

Perfectionists have a whale of a battle with this. They want life to be lived flawlessly by everyone. That is why I have said for years that perfectionists are people who take pains—and give them to others.

If a man as capable as Paul freely admitted he had not arrived, we should have little difficulty saying the same. Nevertheless, progress is the main agenda of life. If you can see changes in your own life as compared to, say, a year ago or more, take heart! You are on the right road.

2. The past is over . . . forget it! The original word Paul used when he wrote, "forgetting what lies behind," was a Greek term that meant fully forgetting, *completely* forgetting. Actually, it was an ancient athletic term used of a runner who outran another in the same race: Once he got into the lead, he would never turn and look back; he would forget about the other runner. The one in the lead focuses on the tape before him rather than the other runners behind him.

Some of the unhappiest people I have ever known are living their lives looking over their shoulder. What a waste! Nothing back there can be changed.

What's in the past? Only two things: great attainments and accomplishments that could either make us proud by reliving them or indifferent by resting on them . . . or failures and defeats that cannot help but arouse feelings of guilt and shame. Why in the world would anyone want to return to that quagmire? I have never been able to figure that one out. By recalling those inglorious, ineffective events of yesterday, our energy is sapped for facing the demands of today. Rehearsing those wrongs, now forgiven in grace, derails and demoralizes us. There are few joy stealers more insidious than past memories that haunt our minds. Paul says to forget the past! Good advice to all who hope to hang tough.

3. The future holds out hope . . . reach for it! I am not the first to point out that Paul may have had in mind the chariot races so popular in the Olympic Games as he wrote of "reaching forward to what lies ahead." He could have been thinking of the chariot racer standing in that small, two-wheeled cart with long, leather reins in his hands, leaning forward to keep his balance. Can you picture it?

The analogy is clear. In this race called life, we are to face forward, anticipating what lies ahead, ever stretching and reaching, making life a passionate, adventurous quest. Life was never meant to be a passive coexistence with enemy forces as we await our heavenly home. But it's easy to do that, especially when we arrive at a certain age (from our mid-fifties on), to sort of shift into neutral and take whatever comes our way.

Let me pause here in midstream and ask you three direct questions:

- Have you left the past—I mean fully moved on beyond it?
- Are you making progress—some kind of deliberate progress with your life?
- Do you passionately pursue some dream—some specific goal?

Robert Ballard suddenly flashes into my mind. Does that name mean anything to you?

Robert Ballard was a man with a quest. He wanted to find the *Titanic*. And on September 1, 1985, he discovered the sunken ship in the North Atlantic, more than 350 miles off the coast of Newfoundland. I get chills when I read his description of the first time he sent down that bright probe light and saw that sight more than two miles below the surface of those cold waters:

> My first direct view of *Titanic* lasted less than two minutes, but the stark sight of her immense black hull towering above the ocean floor will remain forever ingrained in my memory. My lifelong dream was to find this great ship and during the past 13 years the quest for her has dominated my life.[4]

What is your particular quest? For what are you leaning forward? There is something wonderfully exciting about reaching into the future with excited anticipation, and those who pursue new adventures through life stay younger, think better, and laugh louder! I just spoke with a middle-aged man who told me he hopes to teach himself Mandarin, one of the Chinese dialects, so that when he takes an early retirement in a few years he can go to China and teach English as a second language. He was smiling from ear to ear as he shared his plans, and I encouraged him to keep reaching forward for what lies before.

Cynthia and I recently had lunch with a wonderful couple in their thirties who are seriously considering a mid-career change. He will go to seminary and she will go to work to put him through. They have been thinking about it for years. Both are so excited, so motivated. They said we were the first ones to sound enthusiastic; all the others they had mentioned this to were quick to point out all the possible things that could go wrong. All the sacrifices they would have to endure. Why focus on that? I told them to keep reaching forward . . . to pursue their dream. And do I need to mention it? Both were laughing again as they walked away.

- The plan is progress, not perfection.
- The past is over, forget it.
- The future holds out hope, reach for it.

4. The secret is a determined attitude . . . maintain it! Paul specifically mentions having the right attitude. I wrote about this earlier in the book, but perhaps this is a good time to return to it since attitude is such a vital ingredient in the life of anyone who plans to hang tough. Here, the right attitude is important for those who are on the road to maturity . . . who are growing and are ready for the next lesson to be learned.

By the way, I like the gracious way Paul allows others the liberty to grow at their own pace: "If anyone has a different attitude, God will reveal that to him." But as far as the apostle was concerned, hanging tough and maintaining a determined attitude belonged together.

This reminds me of something similar written elsewhere in the New Testament:

> Consider it all joy, my brethren, when you encounter various trials, knowing that the testing of your faith produces endurance. And let endurance have its perfect result, that you may be perfect and complete, lacking in nothing.
>
> *James 1:2–4*

He does not mean that we reach perfection—we have already established that that is not the goal. He has maturity in mind. James says the same thing:

> Dear brothers, is your life full of difficulties and temptations? Then be happy, for when the way is rough, your patience has a chance to grow. So let it grow, and don't try to squirm out of your problems. For when your patience is finally in full bloom, then you will be ready for anything, strong in character, full and complete.
>
> *James 1:2–4 TLB*

I think of the process as a domino effect. Trials and tests come that impact our patience and give it a chance to grow (do they ever!).

As patience begins to develop, strong character is cultivated, moving us ever onward toward maturity. There is no shortcut! But by refusing to squirm out of your problems, you find yourself becoming the man or woman you have always wanted to be. And did you notice that little tidbit of advice? "Then be happy [there's that reminder again!] . . . for when the way is rough . . . you will be ready for anything. . . ." No major change will shock you.

For years all the members of our family lived under the same roof. Even as one after another of our adult children married and moved into their own homes, they still lived nearby. Our lives remained intertwined, and we maintained a close harmony. And then, almost overnight, we were separated. It was as if a bomb exploded and blew us all around the country.

Our older son, Curt, and his wife, Debbie, plus their three children remained nearby. Happily, they were not involved in the wholesale reshuffling of the Swindoll deck. But our older daughter, Charissa, and her husband, Byron, with their two children moved to Atlanta as Byron changed jobs and joined the Ronald Blue Company. Our younger daughter, Colleen, moved to the Chicago area with her husband, Mark, as he began studying for the ministry at Trinity Evangelical Divinity School. And our younger son, Chuck, moved to Orlando to begin his training as a sound engineer at Full Sail Center for the Recording Arts.

All three of those moves happened suddenly within a period of three months . . . boom, boom, boom! As Cynthia and I sat all alone on our sun porch one morning following the sudden scattering of the Swindoll tribe, our heads still swimming in the backwash of it all, we sort of caught our breath and decided that we would neither fight it nor whine about it. We deliberately chose to maintain a good attitude, which meant accepting what had occurred and adjusting to the new challenge of keeping close ties as best we could between Southern California, Chicago, Atlanta, and Orlando.

Since God is sovereign and is in the midst of everything that happens to us, the sudden trial of being so far removed from one another was something we could all endure. And we have. Our long distance phone bill and our travel expenses tell their own tale, I can assure you. But behind it all—on everyone's part—the secret to hanging tough together . . . and loving it has been everyone's attitude. Who knows? We may live to see the day when we're all back in the same geographical region and our home is, once again, filled with wall-to-wall children—*and grandchildren*—and we will long for the peace and quiet we had finally gotten used to! No, just kidding.

It occurred to Cynthia and me recently that we had reared our children to keep a close watch over their attitudes. All through their growing-up years we preached and tried hard to model positive attitudes, cooperative attitudes, willing and happy attitudes. Laughter has always been heard in our home, so why not apply all that now? It has worked wonders! Because of that, I have been particularly grateful for the piece Bob Benson wrote several years ago.

Laughter in the Walls

I pass a lot of houses on my way home—
   some pretty,
     some expensive,
      some inviting—
but my heart always skips a beat
   when I turn down the road
and see my house nestled against the hill.
   I guess I'm especially proud
of the house and the way it looks because
   I drew the plans myself.
It started out large enough for us—
   I even had a study—
two teenaged boys now reside in there.
   And it had a guest room—
my girl and nine dolls are permanent guests.
   It had a small room Peg
had hoped would be her sewing room—
   two boys swinging on the dutch door
have claimed this room as their own.
   So it really doesn't look right now
as if I'm much of an architect.
   But it will get larger again—
one by one they will go away
     to work,
       to college,
     to service,
    to their own houses,
and then there will be room—
   a guest room,

a study,
and a sewing room
for just the two of us.
But it won't be empty—
every corner
every room
every nick
in the coffee table
will be crowded with memories.
Memories of picnics,
parties, Christmases,
bedside vigils, summers,
fires, winters, going barefoot,
leaving for vacation, cats,
conversations, black eyes,
graduations, first dates,
ball games, arguments,
washing dishes, bicycles,
dogs, boat rides,
getting home from vacation,
meals, rabbits, and
a thousand other things
that fill the lives
of those who would raise five.
And Peg and I will sit
quietly by the fire
and listen to the
laughter in the walls.[5]

5. *The need is keeping a high standard . . . together.* Those who hang tough do better when doing so with others. That is especially true in times of severe crisis. As Benjamin Franklin said at the signing of the Declaration of Independence: "We must all hang together, or assuredly we shall all hang separately."[6] And while pulling together we need to keep a high standard. As the apostle wrote to his Philippian friends, "Let us keep living by that same standard."

Agreeing on the same basics while encouraging each other to hang in there day after day is one of the many benefits of locking arms in close friendship with a small group of Christians. The group not only holds us accountable, but also reminds us we are not alone. I have found that I don't get as weary when I pull up close alongside a few like-minded brothers and take the time to cultivate a meaningful relationship. It is practical *and* biblical:

> And let us not lose heart in doing good, for in due time we shall reap if we do not grow weary.
>
> *Galatians 6:9*

> Therefore, my beloved brethren, be steadfast, immovable, always abounding in the work of the Lord, knowing that your toil is not in vain in the Lord.
>
> *1 Corinthians 15:58*

A WORKABLE PLAN FOR EVERYDAY LIVING

Let me see if I can wrap up this chapter in a single statement. Progress is maintained by:

> Forgetting yesterday's glory and grind
> and by
> Focusing on tomorrow's challenging opportunities
> while we
> Keep the right attitude and remember
> we are in it together.

In all honesty, I am convinced that that is a winning game plan for hanging tough . . . and loving it. In fact, I suggest you duplicate that formula on a small sheet of paper or a three-by-five card and tape it to your bathroom mirror or clip it to the sun visor of your car. Repeat it until it gets transferred to your memory and becomes your motto for the month. I have begun doing that, and do you know what? You guessed it—I've started to laugh again . . . even though half the family is still spread across the country.

Let's lock arms and "press on toward the goal for the prize of the upward call of God in Christ Jesus." Is it a deal?

I can still remember sitting as a small boy in a little church in my hometown, El Campo, Texas, listening to those gospel songs sung by some of the simplest and best folks on earth. They were my mom's and dad's Christian friends and family members—people of my simple roots. One song stands out in my memory above all the rest, a refrain seldom heard in most churches today. It is more than a song. It's a prayer that

declares our commitment to enduring the long haul and maintaining a
high standard.

> I'm pressing on the upward way,
> New heights I'm gaining every day;
> Still praying as I onward bound,
> Lord, plant my feet on higher ground.
>
> Lord, lift me up and let me stand,
> By faith, on heaven's table-land,
> A higher plane than I have found;
> Lord, plant my feet on higher ground.[7]

10

It's a Mad, Bad, Sad World, But . . .

RIGHT ABOUT NOW A FEW OF YOU have had it up to here with being told you need to laugh more. All this stuff about being positive and maintaining a good attitude may be starting to wear thin. You might have started to wonder if the two of us—you and I—are living on the same planet. Maybe you are wondering if Swindoll is really in touch with the raw and wicked side of life. If so, let me reassure you—I am.

I live in the Greater Los Angeles area, remember, which is not anyone's idea of a quaint and quiet village filled with caring people living in lovely harmony. Some of the people I am around and some of the sights I see are enough to make me want to get in my car and drive in the other direction. Hopefully, I wouldn't get shot on the freeway trying to get out of town! Acts of violence and the grossest form of criminal behavior are so prevalent that our local television news reporters could easily fill their hour every evening with nothing but that kind of news. Our area is the breeding ground for the full spectrum of human depravity. Sadly, it is here that many cults originate. It is here that one can find every form of pornography, abuse, addiction, and demonic activity, not to mention the ever-present homeless people I see every day. And then there are the tragic emotional breakdowns and marital breakups I hear about on a regular basis. This place is b-a-a-a-a-d!

Do I live on an idyllic island removed from reality where love is abundant and the soft winds of joy blow through the palm trees? Is this the sort of place a person would choose to raise a family who is hoping to escape the harsh realities of a world gone mad? You know better. There are days I would love to pack up and find a nice protected space away from all the noise and nonsense . . . all the fast-lane greed and filthy air . . . all the conflicts and pressures an overcrowded city like ours includes. But then God gets my attention and reminds me that He hasn't called me to Shady Brook Lane where folks sit on the front porch and swing till dark, snapping peas and watching lightning bugs. My world— my mission, my calling—is the city where life gets ugly and people get hostile and kids are exposed to too much too soon. In this area where depravity is relentlessly on display, only the fit survive.

And that is exactly why I've decided to write a book like this. In a world this bad, laughter is the last thing anyone would expect to hear. Trust me, when you laugh in the midst of *this* cesspool environment, people want to know why. "Laughter is hope's last weapon," as I read recently, and I think it is time we put that weapon to use. Out here, only those who are firm in their faith can laugh in the face of tragedy. As Flannery O'Connor wrote:

> Where there is no belief in the soul, there is very little drama. . . . Either one is serious about salvation or one is not. And it is well to realize that the maximum amount of seriousness admits the maximum amount of comedy. Only if we are secure in our beliefs can we see the comical side of the universe.[1]

The Christian is a weird sort, let's face it. We are earthlings, yet the Bible says we are citizens of heaven. This world may not be our home, but it is our residence. Furthermore, we are to live in the world, but we are not to be of the world. And since joy is one of our distinctives, laughter is appropriate even though we are surrounded by all manner of wrong and wickedness. It can get a little confusing, as A. W. Tozer pointed out rather graphically:

> A real Christian is an odd number anyway. He feels supreme love for One whom he has never seen, talks familiarly every day to Someone he cannot see, expects to go to heaven on the virtue of Another, empties himself in order to be full, admits he is wrong so he can be declared right, goes down in order to get up, is strongest when he is weakest, richest when he is poorest, and happiest when he feels worst. He dies so he can live, forsakes in order to have, gives away so he can keep, sees the invisible, hears the inaudible, and knows that which passeth knowledge.[2]

OUR LORD'S STRANGE STRATEGY

In light of all that, doesn't it seem odd of God not to provide an immediate escape route to heaven as soon as we are converted? Why would He leave us in the midst of such an insane, godless setting? I ask you, why? What kind of strange strategy could He have in mind, leaving heaven-bound people riveted to this hell-bound earth?

The answer is worth pursuing, and I don't know of a more qualified source for that answer than Jesus Christ Himself. As I examine His words to His disciples prior to His crucifixion, I find at least three definitive statements that explain what we can expect as we are left on earth.

1. We can have inner peace in the midst of outer pressure and pain. Read Jesus' words slowly and carefully:

> These things I have spoken to you, that you may be kept from stumbling. They will make you outcasts from the synagogue; but an hour is coming for everyone who kills you to think that he is offering service to God.
>
> *John 16:1–2*

> But when He, the Spirit of truth, comes, He will guide you into all the truth; for He will not speak on His own initiative, but whatever He hears, He will speak; and He will disclose to you what is to come.
>
> *John 16:13*

> These things I have spoken to you, that in Me you may have peace. In the world you have tribulation, but take courage; I have overcome the world.
>
> *John 16:33*

If those words mean anything, they provide straight talk about life minus a cushy comfort zone. We won't be sheltered from life's blows. Settle it in your mind once for all: Christians are not supernaturally protected from the blasts, the horrors, the aches, or the pains of living on this globe. Christians can be unfairly treated, assaulted, robbed, raped, and murdered. We can suffer financial reversals, we can be taken advantage of, abused, neglected, and divorced by uncaring mates. Then how can we expect to be joyful, unlike those around us? Because He promises that deep within He will give us peace . . . an unexplainable, illogical inner peace.

2. We are insulated by divine power, yet we are not to live an isolated existence. Again, pay close attention to Jesus' counsel:

These things Jesus spoke; and lifting up His eyes to heaven, He said, "Father, the hour has come; glorify Thy Son, that the Son may glorify Thee, even as Thou gavest Him authority over all mankind, that to all whom Thou hast given Him, He may give eternal life. And this is eternal life, that they may know Thee, the only true God, and Jesus Christ whom Thou hast sent."

John 17:1–3

And I am no more in the world; and yet they themselves are in the world, and I come to Thee. Holy Father, keep them in Thy name, the name which Thou hast given Me, that they may be one, even as We are. While I was with them, I was keeping them in Thy name which Thou hast given Me; and I guarded them, and not one of them perished but the son of perdition, that the Scripture might be fulfilled. But now I come to Thee; and these things I speak in the world, that they may have My joy made full in themselves. I have given them Thy word; and the world has hated them, because they are not of the world, even as I am not of the world. I do not ask Thee to take them out of the world, but to keep them from the evil one.

John 17:11–15

Take another glance at that last statement. Jesus is praying, deliberately asking the Father *not* to remove us from all the earthly garbage, all the daily debris that gathers around this old sin-cursed planet. Then how can any of us ever laugh again? He insulates us! The fires of unrestrained passion may blaze all around us, but He gives us the power of His protective shield to steer us clear of contamination. And don't think the person of the world doesn't notice.

3. We may be unique, but we must be unified. God is pleased with our differences. No two of us are exactly alike, so each person is able to reach out to his or her own sphere of influence. However, our strength comes from our unity.

They are not of the world, even as I am not of the world. Sanctify them in the truth; Thy word is truth. . . . that they may all be one; even as Thou, Father, art in Me, and I in Thee, that they also may be in Us; that the world may believe that Thou didst send Me. . . . I in them, and Thou in Me, that they may be perfected in unity, that the world may know that Thou didst send Me, and didst love them, even as Thou didst love Me.

John 17:16–17, 21, 23

The idea is this: That they (Christians left on earth) may be brought together into a unit—one powerful force for good—in a society weakened by independence and isolation. As people of the world who have no sense of eternal purpose see this unified front, they will realize their own emptiness and seek to find out what makes the difference. What a strategy! All the more reason for Christ's forever family to remain joyfully unified under the authority of His Majesty, King Jesus.

Our world may be a mad, bad, sad place . . . totally out to lunch, spiritually speaking. But impossible to reach and win? Not on your life. Christ's strange strategy is effective because it defies being ignored.

- peace in pressure and pain
- insulated not isolated
- unique but unified

Stop and think. Is it easy to overlook a person who is at peace when you are gripped by panic? And if you are weak within, does someone who seems strangely insulated make you curious? Furthermore, why would anybody laugh in a cesspool society like ours? I repeat, it is an ingenious strategy.

THE CHRISTIAN'S MARCHING ORDERS

All that brings us back to Paul's letter written to his friends in Philippi. He is writing to Christians—peaceful, joyful, strong, insulated people—who live in the real world. He wants them to know how to get a big job done. And so, he tells them, living for Christ means marching in step with His drumbeat.

Brethren, join in following my example, and observe those who walk according to the pattern you have in us. For many walk, of whom I often told you, and now tell you even weeping, that they are enemies of the cross of Christ, whose end is destruction, whose god is their appetite, and whose glory is in their shame, who set their minds on earthly things. For our citizenship is in heaven, from which also we eagerly wait for a Savior, the Lord Jesus Christ; who will transform the body of our humble state into conformity with the body of His glory, by the exertion of the power that He has even to subject all things to Himself.

Therefore, my beloved brethren whom I long to see, my joy and crown, so stand firm in the Lord, my beloved.

Philippians 3:17—4:1

Here I find several helpful tips on how to make our lives count . . . how to do more than sit around, waiting for Christ's return. Four specifics come to my mind as I read Paul's wise counsel.

First, *we need examples to follow.*

Brethren, join in following my example, and observe those who walk according to the pattern you have in us.

Philippians 3:17

The bad news is: Ours is an arduous, long, and sometimes tedious journey through Cesspool Cosmos. And, observe, it is a walk, not a sprint. The good news is: We are not alone on this demanding pilgrimage, which means that some folks we are traveling with make awfully good models to follow. So, follow them!

I like it that while Paul invited believers to follow him, he also acknowledged that others were worth being followed as well. This is a good place to be reminded that no one person on earth is to be our single source of instruction or our only object of admiration. When that happens we can easily get tunnel vision and draw dangerously close to idolizing an individual. We are told to follow others' example but not to focus fully on one person, no matter how godly or gifted he or she may be. Happy and balanced are those in God's army who have several mentors and respect many heroes.

What is it we look for when searching for examples to follow? I like the things Paul listed for Timothy:

But you [Timothy] followed my teaching, conduct, purpose, faith, patience, love, perseverance, persecutions, and sufferings, such as happened to me at Antioch, at Iconium and at Lystra; what persecutions I endured, and out of them all the Lord delivered me! And indeed, all who desire to live godly in Christ Jesus will be persecuted.

2 Timothy 3:10–12

And never forget that those we follow are to be diligent followers of Christ Himself. He remains the Master Mentor.

Be imitators of me, just as I also am of Christ.

1 Corinthians 11:1

Before I leave this subject, let me point out a few practical suggestions for determining your role models:

- Choose your mentors slowly.
- Study their private lives carefully.
- Spend time with them regularly.

Some who make a good public impression may lack solid character qualities behind the scenes. If you ignore that, you can easily be deceived and disillusioned.

I know from personal experience the downside of following such a model. Without getting into details, there was a time when I was young in the faith and terribly vulnerable. A strong leader with a great deal of charisma sort of swept me off my feet. He became my sole source of teaching, and for several years his was the only voice of authority I took seriously. My respect for the man bordered dangerously near idolatry, though I would have denied it at the time. If he was teaching, I was there to drink in every word. His interpretations became my convictions. Even his mannerisms and terminology rubbed off so much that I lost my own sense of confidence and identity; both were bound up in him. Looking back, I also realize I became extremely serious—fanatically serious—about everything. Thankfully, through a chain of events only the Lord could have orchestrated, all that slowly changed. Several subtle things came to the surface, causing me to question the man's private life. And when I challenged some of the things he was teaching, he made it abundantly clear that no one was *ever* to question him. That did it. My respect for the man quickly eroded. More importantly, I realized that I had been looking up to someone who was not the one I should be following, certainly not exclusively. Hard lesson learned, but a good one.

Interestingly, when I broke that fixation, God began to show me many other things I had been blinded to, and His Word brought fresh insights. With my spiritual equilibrium restored, a new sense of perspective returned, along with a sense of humor that had lain dormant too long. In short, it cleared the way for me to become myself rather than a shadow of someone else. Graciously, in the years that followed, God brought me several wonderful mentors, who did indeed follow Christ. Each one has contributed immeasurably to my spiritual growth.

So, learn from my mistake. We need examples (plural!) to follow. As we integrate their godly characteristics into our lives, we become better people.

Second, *we live among many who are enemies of the cross.* This fact keeps us from following every strong personality we meet. "Many," says Paul, "are enemies."

> For many walk, of whom I often told you, and now tell you even weeping, that they are enemies of the cross of Christ, whose end is destruction, whose god is their appetite, and whose glory is in their shame, who set their minds on earthly things.
>
> *Philippians 3:18–19*

Paul is firm, but he is not judgmental. He is committed to the truth, which sometimes hurts. But is he proud of the contrast between himself and those he calls enemies? No. He states that what he is saying makes him weep.

If you and I are ever going to get involved in sharing the joys of knowing and walking with Christ, we must come to terms with the fact that people without Christ in their lives are lost—absolutely and undeniably L-O-S-T.

In fact, Paul gives us one of the clearest and most pointed descriptions of the person who is lost. He or she is:

- *Destined for eternal hopelessness.* That is their future. The reality of hell should be enough to prompt *anyone* to turn to Christ.

- *Driven by sensual appetites.* Anyone who is exposed to the world of the unbeliever soon finds out how up-to-date the counsel of Paul really is. The timeworn motto, "Eat, drink, and be merry" is still very much in vogue. Sensuality is the fuel that lights their fire.

- *Dedicated to material things.* Virtually *everything* draws the lost person toward possessions . . . things that have price tags, things that are tangible, things that can be owned and must be maintained. In the words of Paul, they "set their minds on earthly things."

When all this is added up, is it surprising that the sound of laughter has been drowned out? As you read over the list, you realize anew the emptiness, the boredom of such an existence. No laughter here.

Now the point of this analysis of the lost is not to judge or to condemn or to leave the impression that Christians are better than non-Christians. It is to remind us that God has placed us among them. They are, in fact, in the majority! Our mission is not to argue with them or put them down or make them feel ashamed; it is to reach out to them! To *win* them. To help them realize there is much more to life than they have ever known. To model a different lifestyle that is so convincing, so appealing, that their curiosity will be tweaked, so they might discover what they are missing. The non-Christian world may be lost and running on empty, but they are not stupid or unaware of their surroundings. When they come across an individual who is at peace, free of fear and worry, fulfilled, and genuinely happy, no one has to tell them that something is missing from their lives. Ours may be a mad, bad, sad world, but it is not *blind.* And it is certainly not unreachable. Interesting them in something meaningful and different is not an impossibility. Who doesn't want relief? Freedom from addictions? A purpose for living? A reason to laugh again?

I mentioned earlier that I am engaged in a radio ministry, Insight for Living. Frequently listeners will call and/or write to communicate the changes that have happened in their lives as a result of listening to the broadcasts. We have file drawers full of such letters, each one telling how a person was attracted to the program, often because of what was missing in his or her own life.

I shall never forget one such letter from a young woman who had reached the absolute end of her rope. She had checked into a motel, planning to take her life. Throughout the night she sat on the side of the bed and mentally rehearsed her miserable existence. She had endured numerous failed relationships with men and had had several abortions. She was empty, angry, and could see no reason to go on. Finally, just before dawn, she reached in her purse and pulled out a loaded pistol. Trembling, she stuck it in her mouth and closed her eyes. Suddenly the clock radio snapped on. Apparently the previous occupant had set the radio to come on at that precise time on that precise station . . . and the musical theme of "Insight for Living" filled the room. The uplifting sounds startled her. She tried to ignore it, but couldn't. She heard my voice and found herself strangely attracted to the message of new hope and authentic joy that she had never heard in her entire life. Before the thirty-minute broadcast ended, she gave her life to Jesus Christ. When she contacted us to tell us what had happened, she said she could still taste the cold steel from the gun barrel she had pulled from her mouth.

Not all stories are that dramatic. Some call or write, requesting help to get past the horrible scars of years gone by. Some are victims of abuse. Others write of another kind of emptiness—affluent boredom and materialistic greed, where enough was never enough—but they have nothing else to fill the void. Businessmen and women on a maddening pace to get to the top contact us about their lack of happiness and contentment, their dreadful feelings of distance from their mates and children, and their disillusionment with "the system." Many mention extramarital affairs they are not able to stop or addictions they cannot control: alcoholism, drugs, food, sex.

In each case, it seems, they realize that Christ is able to provide what is missing, and they want to or have entrusted their lives to Him. Most mention their feelings of hopelessness and their inability to help themselves. They long to be free . . . free to live rather than merely exist in a revolving door of repeated defeats . . . free enough to laugh again. It is *that* ingredient we notice in virtually all the letters of transformed lives . . . joy—*outrageous* joy.

Third, *we belong to those who are bound for heaven.*

> For our citizenship is in heaven, from which also we eagerly wait for a Savior, the Lord Jesus Christ; who will transform the body of our humble state into conformity with the body of His glory, by the exertion of the power that He has even to subject all things to Himself.
>
> *Philippians 3:20–21*

Isn't that a great thought? "Our citizenship is in heaven." But let's never forget that our involvements are on earth. That may create a little tension now and then, but what a challenging opportunity! Only heaven-bound people are objective enough to make a major difference on earth. While we "eagerly wait for a Savior," we are able to introduce earth-bound people to a whole new way of life. Can you imagine the curiosity that a bunch of us could arouse just by living lives of relaxed laughter, enjoying delightful fun together? Bystanders would stare in wonder and amazement. They couldn't stand it, being left out. They would *have* to know what they were missing and why we are able to have so much fun, and it would be our joy to tell them. *I love it!* Ours may be a mad, bad, sad old world, but impossible to impact? Get serious! No, on second thought, *get happy!*

I have never been able to figure out why heaven-bound citizens of glory have become so grim. In only a matter of time we shall be transformed from our present condition and conformed into Christ's image—what a change! And in light of that, why is a little temporary period of tough times on earth so all-fired important? It's time we looked different and sounded different. It is time we began to laugh again.

Solomon was absolutely right:

> A joyful heart is good medicine,
> But a broken spirit dries up the bones.
>
> *Proverbs 17:22*

Did you know that laughter actually does work like a medicine in our systems? It exercises our lungs and stimulates our circulation. It takes our minds off our troubles and massages our emotions. Laughter decreases tension. When we laugh, a sort of temporary anesthesia is released within us that blocks the pain as our attention is diverted. As I mentioned earlier, laughter is one of the healthiest exercises we can enjoy. It literally brings healing.

Who hasn't heard about Norman Cousins' remarkable experience? In his excellent book, *Anatomy of an Illness as Perceived by the Patient,* he tells about his battle with an "incurable" disease and the pain he endured as his body's collagen was deteriorating. That, by the way, is the fibrous material that holds the body's cells together. In Cousins' own words, he was "becoming unstuck."

He decided to take matters into his own hands and treat himself (with his doctor's approval) by (1) taking vitamins, (2) eating only healthy food, and—are you ready for this?—(3) undergoing "laugh therapy" by watching old, funny Marx Brothers movies, clips from "Candid Camera," and cartoons . . . and anything else that would make him laugh. He found that if he laughed hard for ten minutes straight, he could enjoy about two hours of relief from pain. To his doctor's amazement, Cousins eventually recovered.[3] The man lived many years beyond anyone's expectations . . . anyone's but his! Norman Cousins' remarkable story reminds me of another of Solomon's proverbs, "The cheerful heart has a continual feast" (Prov. 15:15 NIV).

Think of the impact we could have as earth-free citizens of heaven living hilariously enjoyable, responsible, yet wonderfully carefree lives among people who cannot find anything funny in their shattered world of madness, badness, and sadness. If Laurel and Hardy, the Three Stooges, and the Marx Brothers could help Norman Cousins recover, just think of the healing power that could come from the joy of Jesus Christ. No comparison. But we can't forget the key: You and I . . . we must be the ones who model the message if we ever hope to help our world laugh again. It was G. K. Chesterton who wrote:

> I am all in favor of Laughing. Laughter has something in it in common with the ancient winds of faith and inspiration; it unfreezes pride and unwinds secrecy; it makes men forget themselves in the presence of something greater than themselves; something (as the common phrase goes about a joke) that they cannot resist.[4]

Fourth, *we must stand firm, but not stand still.*

> Therefore, my beloved brethren whom I long to see, my joy and crown, so stand firm in the Lord, my beloved.

Philippians 4:1

Earlier Paul admonished us to "be confident in the Lord" (1:6). Later, to "have the Lord's attitude" (2:5). Next, to "rejoice in the Lord" (3:1). And now he is saying we are to "stand firm in the Lord" (4:1). All the way through the letter to the Philippians the focus has been not on our circumstances or on others or on ourselves, but on the Lord, our source of life and love, confidence and joy.

Here we are being told to "stand firm." But let's not confuse this with standing still. In a world like ours, it is easy to get caught up in the system and lose our stability, hence the command, "Stand firm." In other words, keep your equilibrium . . . don't let the highs and lows sway you . . . get a firm grip on that eternal relationship you have with the Lord and don't let go. He will give you the strength to go on, and He will continue bringing to your attention the thoughts that will keep you positive, affirming, and winsome.

In the final lines of this chapter, I want to encourage you to be all you can be in this world that long ago lost its way. You may not know it and you may not feel like it, but to someone else you are the only source of light and laughter. They may be mad or they may be bad or they may be sad, but, I repeat, they are not unreachable. The real question is this: Are you willing to do the reaching?

It may be a long reach. And sometimes we get our hands slapped . . . our feelings hurt. That's okay. Hurting people often hurt people. But we have God on our side.

So come on out of your shell and reach. Even though the reachable may sometimes act unreachable, keep on reaching. And remember, a good mixture of compassion and realism is essential.

I like the wry comment Barbara Johnson makes in her book, *Splashes of Joy in the Cesspools of Life:*

> The rain falls on the just and also on the unjust, but
> > chiefly on the just,
> Because the unjust steals the just's umbrella.[5]

No problem . . . like I've been saying, it's a mad, bad, sad world. Even if you get wet doing it, keep reaching, and, for sure, keep laughing.

11

Defusing Disharmony

*I*N A PARABLE SHE ENTITLES "A Brawling Bride," Karen Mains paints a vivid scene, describing a suspenseful moment in a wedding ceremony. Down front stands the groom in a spotless tuxedo—handsome, smiling, full of anticipation, shoes shined, every hair in place, anxiously awaiting the presence of his bride. All attendants are in place, looking joyful and attractive. The magical moment finally arrives as the pipe organ reaches full crescendo and the stately wedding march begins.

Everyone rises and looks toward the door for their first glimpse of the bride. Suddenly there is a horrified gasp. The wedding party is shocked. The groom stares in embarrassed disbelief. Instead of a lovely woman dressed in elegant white, smiling behind a lace veil, the bride is limping down the aisle. Her dress is soiled and torn. Her leg seems twisted. Ugly cuts and bruises cover her bare arms. Her nose is bleeding, one eye is purple and swollen, and her hair is disheveled.

"Does not this handsome groom deserve better than this?" asks the author. And then the clincher: "Alas, His bride, THE CHURCH, has been fighting again!"[1]

Calling them (and us) "the church," the apostle Paul writes to the Ephesians:

> Christ . . . loved the church and gave Himself up for her . . . to make her holy and clean . . . so that He could give her to Himself as a glorious church without a single spot or wrinkle or any other blemish, being holy and without a single fault.
>
> *Ephesians 5:25–27 NASB/TLB*

Wonderful plan . . . but hardly a realistic portrayal. I mean, can you imagine what the wedding pictures would look like if Christ claimed

His bride, the church, *today?* Try to picture Him standing next to His brawling bride. It is one thing for us to survive the blows of a world that is hostile to the things of Christ, but to be in disharmony with one another, fighting and arguing among ourselves—unthinkable.

Puritan Thomas Brookes once penned these words: "For wolves to worry lambs is no wonder, but for lambs to worry one another, this is unnatural and monstrous."[2]

Unthinkable and unnatural though it may seem, the bride has been brawling for centuries. We get along for a little while and then we are back at each others' throats. After a bit we make up, walk in wonderful harmony for a few days, then we turn on one another. We can switch from friend to fiend in a matter of moments.

In a "Peanuts" cartoon, Lucy says to Snoopy: "There are times when you really bug me, but I must admit there are also times when I feel like giving you a big hug."

Snoopy replies: "That's the way I am . . . huggable and buggable."

And so it is with us and our relationships within the ranks of God's family. I'm not referring to the variety of our personalities, gifts, tastes, and preferences—that's healthy. The Master made us like that. It's our mistreatment of each other, the infighting, the angry assaults, the verbal misrepresentations, the choosing of sides, the stubborn wills, the childish squabbles. An objective onlooker who watches us from a distance could wonder how and why some of us call ourselves Christians. "Well," you ask, "must we always agree?" No, absolutely not. But my question is this: Why can't we be *agreeable?* What is it that makes us so ornery and nitpicking in our attitudes? Why so many petty fights and ugly quarrels? Why so little acceptance and tolerance? Aren't we given the direct command to "keep the unity of the Spirit in the bond of peace"? What makes Christ's bride forget those words and have so many verbal brawls?

ANALYZING CONFLICT'S CAUSE AND EXTENT

James asked similar questions back in the first century—which tells us that disharmony is not solely a twentieth-century malady. Even back in the days when life was simple and everyone's pace was slower, there were squabbles.

What is the source of quarrels and conflicts among you? Is not the source your pleasures that wage war in your members? You lust and do not have; so you commit murder. And you are envious and cannot obtain; so you fight and quarrel. You do not have because you do not ask. You ask and do not receive, because you ask with wrong motives, so that you may spend it on your pleasures.

James 4:1–3

James never was the type to beat around the bush. With penetrating honesty he asks and answers the critical question. The terms he uses are extremely descriptive: "quarrels and conflicts." The first term is from the Greek word for "war." It conveys a scene of broad and bloody hostility between opposing parties. The second represents smaller skirmishes, local and limited battles, even a chronic state of disharmony. During World War II there were two massive "theaters" of warfare, vast territories on opposite sides of our country: the European theater of war and the Pacific theater of war. Within both numerous skirmishes and individual battles took place. That is the idea here.

The same can be seen to this day within the ranks of religion. England and Ireland have sustained their territorial and denominational "quarrel" for centuries. People on both sides are still being killed and crippled by real bombs and real bullets. Less bloody perhaps, but no less real are the denominational quarrels in our own land—fights and splits within the ranks. Seminaries quarrel as one theological position takes up arms against another. The disputes appear civil and sophisticated as each side publishes its position in journals and books, but behind the veil of intellectualism is a great deal of hostility.

And then there are those "conflicts" between local churches as well as among members of the same church. Small, petty battles . . . arguments, power struggles, envyings, catty comments, silent standoffs, and even lawsuits between members of the body of Christ. These may not be on the national news, but they can get ugly.

A pastor from another state recently told me that some of the members of his board of elders had not spoken to one another for over a year. A concerned board member from a different church in another state said he had recently resigned because he had gotten exhausted from doing nothing but "putting out fires" and "trying to keep church members happy." His particular church had been through two major splits in the past seven years over reasons that would make you smile and shake your head in disbelief. Such are the "conflicts among us."

Why We Have Them

James points to "the source" as he addresses the issue. His answer may seem strange: "Is not the source your pleasures that wage war in your members?"

"Pleasures" doesn't sound very hostile, does it? Maybe not in our English language, but the Greek word is the one from which we get "hedonism." It means the strong desire to get what one does not have, which includes the idea of satisfying oneself . . . the passion to get what one wants, regardless. Such an intense craving drives us to shameful and selfish actions. As James puts it, such pleasures lead us to "wage war"—*strateuo*—from which we get "strategy." Our desire to get what we want prompts us to strategize: to put a plan in motion that will result in *my* getting *my* way.

Is this a determined effort? Look again at what James writes:

> You lust and do not have; so you commit murder. And you are envious and cannot obtain; so you fight and quarrel. You do not have because you do not ask.
>
> *James 4:2*

I'd call that determined! If it calls for a fight, *fight!* If it means an argument, *argue!* If it will require getting other people to back me up, *enlist!* If stronger words will help me reach my objective and get what I want, *murder!*

I realize we don't carry weapons to church—not literally. That is not necessary, since the muscle behind our teeth is always ready to launch its killing missiles. We may not bring blood from another's body, but we certainly know how to make them squirm and hopefully surrender. And we never admit it is because we are selfish or because we crave our own way—there's always a principle at stake or a cause worth fighting for that's bigger than personalities. Sure, sure.

I realize that on a few occasions conflicts will arise. There *are* those times when it is essential to stand one's ground and refuse to compromise biblical principles. But more often than not the nasty infighting among us is embarrassingly petty. And, unfortunately, the world has a field day watching us fight and quarrel for the silliest of reasons.

Ways We Express Our Disharmony

Rationalizing our wrong attitudes and actions, we Christians will go to amazing lengths to get our way. The history of the church is strewn with the litter of battle. I repeat, some of those fights were unselfish and necessary. To have backed away would have meant compromising convictions clearly set forth in the Scriptures. But more often than not the "quarrels and conflicts" have expressed themselves in personal power plays, political maneuvering, strong-minded and selfish parishioners determined to get their own way, stubborn pastors who intimidate and bully others, unbending and tightfisted board members who refuse to listen to reason, and, yes, those who seem to delight in stirring up others through rumor and gossip. It's just a mess! Sometimes I wonder how the Shepherd puts up with us. We can be such wayward, stubborn sheep! And to think He sees it all—each and every cutting word or ugly act—yet loves us still. Only because of His grace are we able to continue on.

Marshall Shelley, in his book *Well-Intentioned Dragons,* talks about disharmony in the church from another perspective. Sometimes it is from folks who don't necessarily mean to be difficult, but they are.

Dragons, of course, are fictional beasts—monstrous reptiles with lion's claws, a serpent's tail, bat wings, and scaly skin. They exist only in the imagination.

But there are dragons of a different sort, decidedly real. In most cases, though not always, they do not intend to be sinister; in fact, they're usually quite friendly. But their charm belies their power to destroy.

Within the church, they are often sincere, well-meaning saints, but they leave ulcers, strained relationships, and hard feelings in their wake. They don't consider themselves difficult people. They don't sit up nights thinking of ways to be nasty. Often they are pillars of the community—talented, strong personalities, deservingly respected—but for some reason, they undermine the ministry of the church. They are not naturally rebellious or pathological; they are loyal church members, convinced they're serving God, but they wind up doing more harm than good.

They can drive pastors crazy . . . or out of the church.

Some dragons are openly critical. They are the ones who accuse you of being (pick one) too spiritual, not spiritual enough, too dominant, too laid back, too narrow, too loose, too structured, too disorganized, or ulterior in your motives.

These criticisms are painful because they are largely unanswerable. How can you defend yourself and maintain a spirit of peace? How can you possibly prove the purity of your motives? Dragons make it hard to disagree without being disagreeable.

Relationships are both the professional and personal priority for pastors—getting along with people is an essential element of any ministry—and when relationships are vandalized by critical dragons, many pastors feel like failures. Politicians are satisfied with 51 percent of the constituency behind them; pastors, however, feel the pain when one vocal member becomes an opponent.

Sightings of these dragons are all too common. As one veteran pastor says, "Anyone who's been in ministry more than an hour and a half knows the wrath of a dragon." Or, as Harry Ironside described it, "Wherever there's light, there's bugs."[3]

LOOKING THROUGH THE KEYHOLE
OF A FIRST-CENTURY CHURCH

I would be a lot more discouraged about the problem of disharmony among believers if I didn't remember that it has been around since the church began. Those early churches were anything but pockets of perfection. Christians in places like Corinth and Galatia, Rome and Thessalonica had their troubles just like those living in towns and cities all around our world today. Even Philippi—as fine a group of Jesus People as they were—had their own skirmishes, one of which Paul pinpointed in his letter to them.

> Therefore, my beloved brethren whom I long to see, my joy and crown, so stand firm in the Lord, my beloved.
> I urge Euodia and I urge Syntyche to live in harmony in the Lord. Indeed, true comrade, I ask you also to help these women who have shared my struggle in the cause of the gospel, together with Clement also, and the rest of my fellow workers, whose names are in the book of life.
>
> *Philippians 4:1–3*

In his typical fashion, Paul starts with a general principle before he addresses a specific concern; then he wraps things up as he makes a request. Behind it all is his unspoken desire that the Philippians defuse the disharmony and begin to laugh again. When disharmony persists, the first thing to go is the sweetest sound that can be heard in a church—

laughter. Perhaps it had been too long since the Philippians had enjoyed the presence of one another. Paul's hope is that once this difficulty is cleared up, their joy might return.

A Primary Principle

Solving problems that grow out of disharmony among believers calls for a return to standing firm in the things of the Lord, not satisfying self.

> Therefore, my beloved brethren whom I long to see, my joy and crown, so stand firm in the Lord, my beloved.
>
> *Philippians 4:1*

Earlier in the letter Paul had written:

> Only conduct yourselves in a manner worthy of the gospel of Christ; so that whether I come and see you or remain absent, I may hear of you that you are standing firm in one spirit, with one mind striving together for the faith of the gospel.
>
> *Philippians 1:27*

Actually, the idea of standing firm is one of the apostle's favorite topics. For example:

"Stand firm in the faith" (1 Cor. 16:13).
"Keep standing firm" (Gal. 5:1).
"Now we really live, if you stand firm in the Lord" (1 Thess. 3:8).
"So then, brethren, stand firm" (2 Thess. 2:15).

Why place such an emphasis on standing firm in the Lord? What's the big deal? Let me suggest to you that it is one of the most foundational principles of maintaining harmony:

STANDING FIRM IN THE LORD

PRECEDES

RELATING WELL IN THE FAMILY

What would standing firm include? Following Christ's teachings. Respecting His Word. Modeling His priorities. Loving His people.

Seeking and carrying out His will. It has been my observation that those who are committed to these things have little difficulty relating well to other members of God's family. Not surprisingly the very next issue Paul brings up has to do with two in the church at Philippi who needed to "live in harmony" with one another. But before I go into that, this might be a good time for you to ask yourself, "Am I one who stands firm *in the Lord?*" Other options create havoc: Standing firm *for what I want* . . . or, standing firm *in honor of tradition* . . . or, standing firm *with a couple of my friends.*" Unquestionably, those three positions represent the antithesis of "standing firm in the Lord."

A Relational Need

Having stated the principle, Paul puts his finger on the specific conflict at Philippi. He even names names.

> I urge Euodia and I urge Syntyche to live in harmony in the Lord.
>
> *Philippians 4:2*

Let me mention several observations:

1. These are two women in the church at Philippi (feminine names).
2. They are mentioned nowhere else in the Scriptures.
3. The specific details of their dispute are not explained.
4. Paul's counsel is to urge them toward harmony: "I urge . . . I urge" (he neither rebukes them nor pontificates).
5. He appeals to their conscience . . . their hearts (intrinsic motivation).

I am just as impressed with what Paul does not do.

He does not spell out a step-by-step process; that was for the two women to work out on their own. Equally impressive, he does not pull rank by adding a warning or a threat, like, "I'll give you two weeks to clear this up," or "If you don't straighten up, I will. . . ."

Paul handled the matter with dignity and grace. While he was deeply concerned ("I urge . . . I urge"), he did not attempt to take charge of the situation from a distance. If anyone is tempted to think Paul was too passive or should have said more, a quick reading of other renderings may help:

- "I plead with . . . I plead with . . ." (NIV).
- "Please, please, with the Lord's help, quarrel no more—be friends again." (TLB).
- "Euodias and Syntyche, I beg you by name to make up your differences as Christians should!" (PHILLIPS).

By repeating the verb ("I urge . . . I urge"), Paul leaves the impression that there was fault on both sides. In fact, the Vulgate, the Latin version of Scripture, uses different verbs in the appeal, which seems to emphasize mutual wrong.

I have seldom seen an exception to this: When disharmony arises between two people or two groups, there is some measure of fault on both sides. The road leading to a breakdown in harmony is never a one-way street. Both parties must be encouraged to see each other's fault, each other's failure . . . and meet on common ground with a mutual willingness to listen and to change.

And what is that common ground? The statement Paul makes includes the answer: "live in harmony in the Lord." Just as we are to "stand firm" in Him, so are we to find agreement in Him. Both sides need to make Him their focus if a solution is ever going to be found. It is as if the Apostle of Grace is saying, "It is important that both release their grudge and state their forgiveness and adopt the same attitude as their Lord when He unselfishly came from heaven to earth to be our Savior. Only then will there be renewed harmony."

One more thought before moving on. Everything we know of these two women is: They quarreled. Down through the centuries the only answer that could be given to the question: "Who were Euodia and Syntyche?" has been "They were two women from Philippi who lived in disharmony." That prompts me to ask you: If *your* life were to be summed up in a single statement, what would that statement be?

An Affirming Request

Occasionally a dispute is so deep and longstanding that it calls for a third party—an objective, unprejudiced arbitrator—to come between those in conflict to help bring restoration. That is Paul's request here:

> Indeed, true comrade, I ask you also to help these women who have shared my struggle in the cause of the gospel, together with Clement also, and the rest of my fellow workers, whose names are in the book of life.

Philippians 4:3

All sorts of suggestions have been made as to the identity of the one called "true comrade." One scholar suggested Barnabas. If so, why didn't Paul call him by name? Another said it could have been Epaphroditus. But, again, one wonders why he would have been called by name earlier yet referred to as "true comrade" here. A curious suggestion has been a person named Sunzugos, which is the Greek transliteration of "comrade." One fanciful idea is that the person was one of their husbands (I doubt that either husband would have relished that role) . . . another, that it was Paul's wife!

The name of the mediator is not nearly as important as the help that he or she could bring ("help these women"). Why did this mean so much to Paul that he included it in his letter? Because these women were important. They had "shared in the struggle" with Paul, and they belonged to the same spiritual family. Their clash was hurting the fellowship among the Christians at Philippi, so it needed resolution . . . soon. The bride needed to stop brawling!

Someone has said that Christians trying to live in close harmony is the next thing to impossible. The scene is not unlike the old forest folktale where two porcupines were huddled close together on a cold, cold night up in northern Canada. The closer they got to stay warm, the more their quills pricked each other, making it virtually impossible for them to remain side by side. Silently, they scooted apart. Before long, they were shivering in the wintry gale, so they came back together. Soon both were poking and jabbing each other . . . so they separated again. Same story . . . same result. Their action was like a slow-moving, monotonous dance—back and forth, back and forth.

Those two women in Philippi were like the Canadian porcupines; they needed each other, but they kept needling each other. Unfortunately, the disruptive dance of disharmony did not stop in that first-century church.

May I speak to you heart-to-heart, as friend-to-friend, before ending this chapter? In all honesty, have my words opened an old wound that has never healed? Did the imaginary scene of a brawling bride bring back a few ugly memories of an unresolved conflict in your past . . . or maybe several of them? Is there someone you continue to blame for the hurt you had to endure, bringing pain that never got reconciled? If so, do you have any idea how much emotional energy you are burning up nursing that wound? And while I'm asking questions: Are you aware of the joy-stealing effect an unforgiving spirit is having on your life? If your bitterness is deep enough, you've virtually stopped living. It is no wonder you have also stopped laughing!

Please listen to me. *It is not worth it.* You need to come to terms with this lingering, nagging issue *now.* The peace and contentment and joy that could be yours are draining away, like water down the drain of an unplugged bathtub. It is time for you to call a halt to the dispute; the disharmony must be defused. But it won't happen automatically. You are an essential part of the healing equation. You must do something about it.

Start by telling God how much it hurts and that you need Him to help you to forgive the offense. If you have a friend who is close enough to you to help you work your way through the process, reach out and say so. Get rid of all the poison of built-up anger and pour out all the acid of long-term resentment. Your objective is clear: Fully forgive the offender. Once that is done, you will discover that you no longer rehearse the ugly scenes in your mind. The revengeful desire to get back and get even will wane, and in its now-empty space will come such an outpouring of relief and a new spirit of joy that you won't feel like the same person. That deep frown on your brow and those long lines on your face will slowly disappear. And before too long you will get reacquainted with a sound you haven't made for months, maybe years. It is called laughter.

A resentful, unforgiving spirit and a carefree, happy heart never existed in the same body. Until you take care of the former you won't be able to enjoy the latter.

CONSIDERING THE LESSONS THIS TEACHES US . . .

I can think of at least four practical lessons we have learned from the things we have been considering.

1. Clashes will continue to occur. I wish I could promise you otherwise, but as long as depravity pollutes humanity, we can forget about a

conflict-free environment. So, don't be surprised when another skirmish breaks out.

2. Not all conflicts are wrong. Not all disagreements require reconciliation. As I recall, it was Jesus who said that He brings "a sword" into certain relationships. Occasionally it is right to be defiant and to fight. When critical biblical lines are drawn and the issues at stake have nothing to do with personal preferences or individual personalities, surrendering to a cause that would lead to wrong is wrong.

3. If the disagreement *should* be resolved and *could* be resolved but is not, then stubbornness and selfishness are at the core. We may be adults in age and height, but we can be awfully childish in attitude. Come on, give in. To persist in this lack of harmony brings hurts far greater than the small radius of your relationship.

4. Should you be the "comrade" needed to assist in the reconciliation, remember the threefold objective:

- The ultimate goal: Restoration (not discipline)
- The overall attitude: Grace (not force)
- The common ground: Christ (not logic or the church or tradition or your will)

There is something magnanimous about the name of Jesus that softens our attitude and defuses disharmony. Somehow the insertion of His name makes it inappropriate to maintain a fighting spirit.

The truth of that was underscored when I read of something that happened over one hundred years ago.

Charles H. Spurgeon, Baptist minister of London, England, had a pastor-friend, Dr. Newman Hall, who wrote a book entitled, *Come to Jesus.* Another preacher published an article in which he ridiculed Hall, who bore it patiently for a little while. But when the article gained popularity, Hall sat down and wrote a letter of protest. His answer was full of retaliatory invectives that outdid anything in the article which attacked him. Before mailing the letter, Hall took it to Spurgeon for his opinion.

Spurgeon read it carefully then, handing it back, asserted it was excellent and that the writer of the article deserved it all. "But," he added, "it just lacks one thing." After a pause Spurgeon continued,

"Underneath your signature you ought to write the words, 'Author of *Come to Jesus.*'"

The two godly men looked at each other for a few minutes. Then Hall tore the letter to shreds.[4]

12

*Freeing Yourself Up
to Laugh Again*

CYNTHIA AND I ARE INTO Harley-Davidson motor-cycles.

I know, I know . . . it doesn't fit our image. Who really cares? We stopped worrying about our image years ago. We should be ashamed of ourselves? We aren't. We're having a mutual mid-life crisis? We hope so. We should be better examples to the youth? They love it! Actually, it's only a few crotchety adults who don't. What are we going to say to our grandkids? "Hey, kids, wanna ride?" And how are we supposed to explain it to "the board?" They don't care either. This is *California*, remember?

We are having more fun than anybody can imagine (except fellow Harley riders). One of the best things about the whole deal is that those guys and gals down at the bike shop don't have a clue as to who we are. We have *finally* found a place in our area where we can be out in public and remain absolutely anonymous. If anybody down there happens to ask our names, we'll just tell 'em we're Jim and Shirley Dobson. Those Harley hogs don't know them either.

You should have been in the showroom when I first sat on one of those big bikes. Cynthia stood a few feet away and just stared. She didn't know whether to laugh out loud or witness to me. She compromised and hopped on behind after I winked at her. She couldn't resist. As soon as she leaned forward and whispered in my ear, "Honey, I could get used to this," I knew it wouldn't be long before we'd be truckin' down the asphalt without a worry in the world.

We sat there and giggled like a couple of high school sweethearts sipping a soda through two straws. She liked the feel of sitting close to me (she couldn't resist, naturally), and I liked the feel of her behind me and that giant engine underneath us. And that inimitable Harley *roar*. Man, it was great!

Suddenly, sitting on that shiny black Heritage Softail Classic with thick leather saddlebags, we were on the back streets of Houston in 1953 all over again, roaring our way to a Milby High School football game. She was wearing my letterman's sweater and red-and-white saddle ox-fords, and I had a flattop with a ducktail and a black leather jacket with fringe and chrome studs!

When we came back to our senses, we realized that somehow we were sorta misfits. I mean, a responsible senior pastor and radio preacher in a suit and tie with a classy, well-dressed woman who is executive vice president of Insight for Living perched on a Harley-Davidson in a mo-torcycle showroom. Everybody else was wearing t-shirts, torn jeans, boots, black leather stuff, and sported tattoos. I saw one guy who had a tattoo on each arm . . . one was of a snarling bulldog with a spiked col-lar and the other was the Marine insignia—the eagle, globe, and anchor of the Corps! A few folks were glancing in our direction as if to say, "Get serious!" And Cynthia leaned up again and whispered, "Do you think we ought to be in here?"

"Of course, honey, who cares? After all, *I'm a Marine!* What I need is a pair of black jeans and leather chaps and all you need is a tattoo, and we'll blend right in." The jeans and chaps for me, probably someday. But Cynthia with a tattoo? I rather doubt it. Somehow I don't think it would go over very big at formal church dinners and the National Religious Broadcasters banquets.

We have had one hilarious time with this in our family. Espe-cially since I raised all four of our kids with only one unchangeable Swindoll rule: "You will not *ever* ride on or own a motorcycle!" Now the old man and his babe are roaring all around town. And it's our now-grown kids who are trying to figure out what's happened to their parents and what to say to *their* kids when they see their grandpar-ents tooling down the freeway like a couple of gray-haired teenagers. Actually, we're getting concerned lately that our children may be a little too strict with *their* kids. "Ya gotta lighten up, guys," as they say down at the Harley hangout. The only one of the bunch who fully understands is our youngest, Chuck—but that makes sense. He rides a Harley too.

What's happening? What would ever possess me to start messing around with a motorcycle, cruising some of the picturesque roads down by the ocean, or taking off with my son for a relaxed, easygoing two or three hours together? What's this all about?

It's about forgetting all the nonsense that every single moment in life is serious. It's about breaking the thick and rigid mold of predictability. It's about enjoying a completely different slice of life where I don't have to concern myself with living up to anyone else's expectations or worry about who thinks what. It's about being with one of our kids in a world that is totally on his turf (for a change), not mine, in a setting that is just plain fun, not work. It's about being me, nobody else.

It's about breaking the bondage of tunnel vision. It's about refusing to live my life playing one note on one instrument in one room and finding pleasure in a symphony of sounds and sights and smells. It's about widening the radius of a restrictive and demanding schedule where breathing fresh air is sometimes difficult and thinking creative thoughts is occasionally the next thing to impossible.

Bottom line, it's about freedom. That's it, plain and simple. It's about being free.

It's about entering into a tension-free, worry-free world where I don't have to say something profound or fix anyone or do anything other than feel the wind and smell the flowers and hug my wife and laugh till we're hoarse. That's it in a nutshell . . . it's about freeing ourselves up to laugh again.

In Jesus' day He took His twelve disciples across a lake to enjoy some R&R alone on a mountainside. Who knows what they did for fun? Maybe they climbed rocks or swam in a cool lake or sat around a campfire and told a few jokes. Whatever, you can count on this—they laughed. Today, Cynthia and I prefer to hop on the old Harley. If Jesus lived on earth today, He might ride with us. But something in me says He probably wouldn't get a tattoo. Then again, who knows? He did a lot of other stuff that made the legalists squirm. He knew the truth . . . and the truth had really set Him free.

GETTING SERIOUS ABOUT BEING SET FREE

Americans did not invent the idea of freedom. Even though we have fought wars for it and built monuments to it, it is not original with us. It began with God, way back in the Garden of Eden when He made Adam and Eve. God made them—and He has made you and me—to enjoy the pleasures and the responsibilities of freedom. How?

- God made us with a mind . . . that we might think freely.
- God made us with a heart . . . that we might love freely.
- God made us with a will . . . that we might obey freely.

Let me analyze those three factors from a strictly human viewpoint. By making us in His image, God gave us capacities not given to other forms of life. Ideally, He made us to know Him, to love Him, and to obey Him. He did not put rings in our noses that He might pull us around like oxen, nor did He create us with strings permanently attached to our hands and feet like human marionettes to control and manipulate our every move. What pleasure would He have in the love of a puppet or the obedience of a dumb animal?

No, He gave us freedom to make choices. By His grace we are equipped to understand His plan because we have a mind with which we can know Him. We are also free to love and adore Him because we have emotions. He takes pleasure in our affection and devotion. We can obey His instructions, but we are not pawns on a global chessboard. It is in the voluntary spontaneity of our response that He finds divine pleasure. When His people *freely* respond in worship and praise, obedience and adoration, God is glorified to the maximum.

There is a downside to all this, however. Because we are free to do these things, we are also free *not* to do them. We are free to make wrong choices—how well we know! In fact, we can continue to make them for so long we can wind up in our own self-made prison of consequences. That prison of our own choosing can hold us in such bondage that we are unable to escape. When that occurs, we experience the ultimate in earthly misery. It is called *addiction*. If you have ever been in such bondage or worked with someone who is, you know firsthand how horrible an existence it can be. Strange as it may seem, an addiction is the tragic consequence of freedom . . . freedom out of control . . . freedom gone to seed.

What God Has Promised

It is at this point that God is ultragracious. He takes no cruel delight in seeing us squirm, trapped in a dungeon of our own making. In fact, that is a large part of the reason He sent His Son to this earth. He sent Him on a mission of mercy to set the captives free. One of the earliest declarations of Christ's Great Commission (His mission statement) is found in Isaiah's ancient prophecy. Though written seven centuries before His birth, this was the coming Messiah's "job description":

> The Spirit of the Lord GOD is upon me,
> Because the LORD has anointed me
> To bring good news to the afflicted;
> He has sent me to bind up the brokenhearted,
> To proclaim liberty to captives,
> And freedom to prisoners;
> To proclaim the favorable year of the LORD,
> And the day of vengeance of our God;
> To comfort all who mourn,
> To grant those who mourn in Zion,
> Giving them a garland instead of ashes,
> The oil of gladness instead of mourning,
> The mantle of praise instead of a spirit of fainting.
> So they will be called oaks of righteousness,
> The planting of the LORD, that He may be glorified.
>
> *Isaiah 61:1–3*

Don't miss those words, "To proclaim liberty to captives and freedom to prisoners."

Lest you think the prophet was writing of himself, notice what Jesus did and said more than seven hundred years later when He was beginning His ministry in Nazareth. Read these words carefully as you imagine the scene:

> And He came to Nazareth, where He had been brought up; and as was His custom, He entered the synagogue on the Sabbath, and stood up to read. And the book of the prophet Isaiah was handed to Him. And He opened the book, and found the place where it was written,
>
> > "THE SPIRIT OF THE LORD IS UPON ME,
> > BECAUSE HE ANOINTED ME TO PREACH THE GOSPEL TO
> >   THE POOR.
> > HE HAS SENT ME TO PROCLAIM RELEASE TO THE
> >   CAPTIVES,
> > AND RECOVERY OF SIGHT TO THE BLIND,
> > TO SET FREE THOSE WHO ARE DOWNTRODDEN,
> > TO PROCLAIM THE FAVORABLE YEAR OF THE LORD."

And He closed the book, and gave it back to the attendant, and sat down; and the eyes of all in the synagogue were fixed upon Him. And He began to say to them, "Today this Scripture has been fulfilled in your hearing."

Luke 4:16–21

Isn't that interesting? Of all the Scriptures He could have read, Jesus selected that section from Isaiah. He not only stated that "release to the captives" and "setting free those who are downtrodden" were on His earthly agenda, but that He was beginning to fulfill Isaiah's prophecy that very day.

Hundreds of years before the Messiah came, God promised that He would set the captives free. Obviously He wasn't referring to opening all prison doors and breaking the bars on every jail. The captives He had in mind were those in bondage to sin. And He also stated that He would provide sight for the blind, physically and spiritually. What grand promises!

Let's glance briefly at one more New Testament scene.

Jesus therefore was saying to those Jews who had believed Him, "If you abide in My word, then you are truly disciples of Mine; and you shall know the truth, and the truth shall make you free." They answered Him, "We are Abraham's offspring, and have never yet been enslaved to anyone; how is it that You say, 'You shall become free'?" Jesus answered them, "Truly, truly, I say to you, everyone who commits sin is the slave of sin. And the slave does not remain in the house forever; the son does remain forever. If therefore the Son shall make you free, you shall be free indeed."

John 8:31–36

What I find significant is the promise from Jesus' lips; namely, that a knowledge of the truth is freeing . . . and once freed, we "shall be free indeed." This refers to a deeply personal freedom, an inner emancipation from what has bound you long enough. What a marvelous thought!

How We Have Responded

If the truth could be known, we have only halfheartedly believed God's promise to us. Even though He has made us to be free and to be released from whatever binds us, many have chosen to live enslaved. By opting for bad choices, they have given all sorts of addictions opportunity to take control. And instead of enjoying the benefits of freedom, many live in its backwash as helpless, hopeless captives.

Jean Jacques Rousseau, the eighteenth-century French philosopher, was never more correct than when he said, "Man was born free, and everywhere he is in chains."[1]

THE MOST UNIVERSAL OF ALL ADDICTIONS

It is time to get specific. So far I have dealt in generalities and not once zeroed in on any one addiction, so you probably feel safe. No longer. Lest you and I start to feel a little smug, thinking we are safe because we don't have a habit so captivating that we are held in bondage, I might as well go to the one addiction that tops all others—worry. Anxiety addicts abound!

The trouble with worry is that it doesn't seem all that harmful. It is a little like the first few snorts of cocaine. A person may know down inside it is not good, but surely it can't be as bad as some have made it out to be. Foolish thinking.

When it comes to worry, we blithely excuse it. For example, one evening we say to a friend, "Hey, don't worry," Our friend responds, "Well, maybe I shouldn't, but you know me. I'm just the worrying type." We answer back, "Yeah, well, I sure understand. I myself am a worrier. Can't blame somebody for feeling a little concerned tonight."

What if we changed that conversation to refer to drinking too much alcohol. Imagine this: "Hey, things will work out." Our friend responds, "Well, maybe I shouldn't, but you know me. I'm just the liquor-drinking type." Answering back, we say, "Yeah, well, I sure understand. I myself drink too much. Can't blame somebody for drinking a couple extras tonight." Suddenly, worry takes on a new significance.

Analyzing the Problem

Of all the joy stealers that can plague our lives, none is more nagging, more agitating, or more prevalent than worry.

We get our English word *worry* from the German word *wurgen,* which means "to strangle, to choke." Our Lord mentioned that very word picture when He addressed the subject on one occasion.

The sower sows the word. And these are the ones who are beside the road where the word is sown; and when they hear, immediately Satan comes and takes away the word which has been sown in them. And in a similar way these are the ones on whom seed was sown on the rocky places, who, when they hear the word, immediately receive it with joy; and they have no firm root in themselves, but are only temporary; then, when affliction or persecution arises because of the word, immediately they fall away. And others are the ones on whom seed was sown among the thorns; these are the ones who have heard the word, and the worries of the world, and the deceitfulness of riches, and the desires for other things enter in and choke the word, and it becomes unfruitful.

Mark 4:14–19

In other words, when worry throttles our thinking, choking out the truth, we are unable to bear fruit. Along with becoming mentally harassed and emotionally strung out, we find ourselves spiritually strangled. Worry cuts off our motivation and lifeline of joy.

In spite of all these consequences, more people are addicted to worry than all other addictions combined. Are you one of them? If you are, you might as well put on hold all the things I have been saying in this book about being more joyful and carefree with an optimistic attitude. You will need to come to terms with your anxiety addiction before you find yourself freed up enough to laugh again.

I know what I'm writing about, believe me. There was a time in my own life when worry controlled me and the tentacles of tension choked much of the fun out of my life. I cared too much about what people thought and said, so I ran a little scared on a daily basis. And then I wasn't sure about my future either. So I worried about that. The churning intensified after I joined the Marines. Cynthia and I had not been married very long. Where would we be stationed? What if I got sent overseas? How would Cynthia do without me . . . and vice versa? The worry list grew once I got my orders—*Okinawa!* Why would God allow this to happen? I mean, the recruiting office promised me that would *never* happen (you're smiling, right?). One by one, day after day, my worries intensified as my joy faded. Prayer was only a formality.

It was while Cynthia and I were separated by the Pacific Ocean for well over a year that I was forced to come to terms with my anxiety addiction. I finally determined to stop that nonsense. I began taking God and His Word much *more* seriously and myself a lot *less* seriously (we usually get those two reversed). I found that prayer was never meant to be a ritual but an actual calling out to God for help . . . and each time I did, He came through. I also discovered that He was in control of life's circumstances as well as the details of my life and my wife. In fact, she was in better care under His sheltering wings than she ever could have been under my roof. She and I both did just fine; matter of fact, *incredibly well.* I kept a journal and I also wrote her letters, sometimes four or five a week. Looking back, I realize it was in the midst of that lonely, involuntary separation that I began to cultivate an interest in writing. (Who would have ever guessed what that letter writing in a little Quonset hut at Camp Courtney, not far from Naha, Okinawa, would lead to?) As I gave my anxieties to God, He took them and solved every one of the things I placed in His care. As I relaxed the tension, He moved in with sovereign grace. It was *wonderful.*

The major turning point occurred when I did an in-depth study of Philippians 4:4–9, which I can still vividly remember. It was then I began . . .

Understanding God's Therapy

Do you realize that God has a sure-cure solution to worry? Has anyone ever told you that if you perfect the process you will be able to live a worry-free existence? Yes, you read that correctly. And if you know me fairly well, you know that I seldom make statements anywhere near that dogmatic. But in this one I am confident. If you will follow God's stated procedure, you will free yourself to laugh again.

First, let's let the Scriptures speak for themselves:

> Rejoice in the Lord always; again I will say, rejoice! Let your forbearing spirit be known to all men. The Lord is near. Be anxious for nothing, but in everything by prayer and supplication with thanksgiving let your requests be made known to God. And the peace of God, which surpasses all comprehension, shall guard your hearts and your minds in Christ Jesus.
>
> *Philippians 4:4–7*

Next, let's get six words clearly fixed in our minds. These six words form the foundation of God's therapeutic process for all worrywarts.

WORRY ABOUT NOTHING,
PRAY ABOUT EVERYTHING

199

Say that over and over until you can say it without looking. Say the six words aloud. Close the book. Close your eyes. Picture the words in your mind. Spend a minute or more turning them over in your head. What qualifies as a worry? Anything that drains your tank of joy—something you cannot change, something you are not responsible for, something you are unable to control, something (or someone) that frightens and torments you, agitates you, keeps you awake when you should be asleep. All of that now needs to be switched from your worry list to your prayer list. Give each worry—one by one—to God. Do that at this very moment. Tell the Lord you will no longer keep your anxiety to yourself.

Now then, once you buy into this all-important plan God has provided for those who wish to be free, you will begin to have time left in your day . . . lots of extra time and energy. Why? Because you used to spend that time worrying. Your addiction, like all addictions, held you captive. It took your time, it required your attention, it forced you to focus on stuff you had no business trying to deal with or solve.

So what now? How do you spend the time you used to waste worrying? Go back to the words from Paul to the Philippians. As I read them over, I find three key words emerging:

. . . **rejoice** (v. 4)

. . . **relax** (v. 5)

. . . **rest** (v. 7)

They look pretty easy, but for someone who has worried as long as *you* have, they are not. You haven't done much of any of these three lately, have you?

To begin with, REJOICE! Worry about nothing . . . pray about everything, and *REJOICE!*

Rejoice in the Lord always; again I will say, rejoice!

Philippians 4:4

Because we have repeated the term and several synonyms throughout the book so often, the whole idea could begin to lose its edge. Don't let it. Rejoicing is clearly a scriptural command. To ignore it, I need to remind you, is disobedience. In place of worry, start spending time enjoying the release of your humor. Find the bright side, the sunny side of life. Deliberately look for things that are funny during your day.

Loosen up and laugh freely. Laugh more often. Consciously stay aware of the importance of a cheerful countenance. Live lightheartedly! Stop reading only the grim sections of the newspaper. Watch less television and start reading more books that bring a smile instead of a frown. That's exactly why you picked up this one! We put a cover on it that would attract your attention (I think my publisher did a bang-up job, don't you?), and as you thumbed through it you probably thought something like, *I need to quit being so serious—maybe this book will help*. Don't stop with this book. Choose others like it. Feed your mind more uplifting "thought food."

Locate a few acquaintances who will help you laugh more at life. Ideally, find Christian friends who see life through Christ's eyes, which is in itself more encouraging. Have fun together. Share funny stories with each other. Affirm one another.

> Shared laughter creates a bond of friendship. When people laugh together, they cease to be young and old, master and pupils, worker and driver. They have become a single group of human beings, enjoying their existence.[2]

Fred Allen, one of my favorite humorists of yesteryear, used to say that it was bad to suppress your laughter because when you do, he said, it goes down and spreads your hips.[3] Maybe that explains those extra pounds.

Solomon writes that "a cheerful heart has a continual feast" (Prov. 15:15), and he is right. I find that a spirit of cheer spreads rapidly. Before you know it, others have joined you at the table. Choose joy! There are very few days in my life during which I find nothing to laugh at. Laughter is the most familiar sound in the hallway where my staff and I work alongside each other. And what a contagious thing is outrageous joy . . . everybody wants to be around it. So, rejoice!

Next, RELAX! Worry about nothing . . . pray about everything, and *RELAX!*

> Let your forbearing spirit be known to all men. The Lord is near.
>
> *Philippians 4:5*

Where do I find "relax" in Paul's statement? See that unusual expression, "forbearing spirit"? It means "gentleness," or "easy." We would say "easygoing." It is "sweet reasonableness" . . . the idea of a relaxed, easygoing lifestyle. A worry-filled world can increase your tension to a dangerous level. Physically, it can take a serious toll on your health.

Lighten up! So much of what we get nervous about and jumpy over never happens anyway. Let me get downright specific. Relax more with your children. Take it easy, especially if they are junior highers (whom my friend, Kenny Poure, calls "pre-people"). If your son or daughter is struggling through a stage in the stormy adolescent years, have a heart. Back off. Loosen the strings. You will realize later that God was there all along—in control—taking care of business, His business. Oh, if only I had applied more of this when our children were younger. Every once in a while, during one of my unrelaxed, high-tension, tightwire acts, one of our kids would say, "Just take a deep breath, Dad." Ouch! When I took their advice, my "forbearing spirit" resurfaced.

My dear friend, Ruth Harms Calkin, describes our dilemma with this insightful reminder:

Spiritual Retreat

This was my calculated plan:
I would set aside my usual schedule—
The menial tasks that wedge in routinely.
In the peace and quiet of my living room
I would relax in Your glorious presence.
How joyfully I envisioned the hours—
My personal spiritual retreat!
With Bible and notebook beside me
I would study and meditate—
I would intercede for the needy world.

But how differently it happened, Lord:
Never has the phone rung so persistently.
Sudden emergencies kept pouring in
Like summer cloudbursts.
My husband came home ill.
There were appointments to cancel
Plans to rearrange.
The mailman brought two disturbing letters
A cousin whose name I couldn't remember
Stopped by on her way through town.
My morning elation became drooping deflation.

And yet, dear Lord
You were with me in it all!
I sense Your vital presence—
Your sure and steady guidance.
Not once did You leave me stranded.
Perhaps, in Your great wisdom
You longed to teach me a practical truth:
When *You* are my Spiritual Retreat
I need not be a spiritual recluse.[4]

And then, REST! Worry about nothing . . . pray about everything, and *REST!*

> Be anxious for nothing, but in everything by prayer and supplication with thanksgiving let your requests be made known to God. And the peace of God, which surpasses all comprehension, shall guard your hearts and your minds in Christ Jesus.

Philippians 4:6–7

I know of few Scriptures that have helped me more than the words you just read. Go back and read them once again, this time slower. Maybe seeing them in The Living Bible will help. That's where I picked up the idea of resting.

> Don't worry about anything; instead, pray about everything; tell God your needs and don't forget to thank him for his answers. If you do this you will experience God's peace, which is far more wonderful than the human mind can understand. His peace will keep your thoughts and your hearts quiet and at rest as you trust in Christ Jesus.

Philippians 4:6–7 TLB

Paul writes of God's peace which "shall guard your hearts and your minds." When he mentions peace as a "guard," he uses a military term for "marching sentry duty" around something valuable and/or strategic. As we rest our case, as we transfer our troubles to God, "Corporal Peace" is appointed the duty of marching as a silent sentry around our minds and our emotions, calming us within. How obvious will it be to others? Go back and check—it will "surpass all comprehension." People simply will not be able to comprehend the restful peace we will model. In place of anxiety—that thief of joy—we pray. We push the worrisome, clawing, monster of pressure off our shoulders and hand it over to God in prayer. I am not exaggerating; I must do that hundreds of times every year. And I cannot recall a time when it didn't provide relief. In its place, always, comes a quietness of spirit, a calming of the mind. With a relieved mind, rest returns.

Rejoice. Relax. Rest. The three substitutes for worry. And impatience. And turmoil.

Correcting Our Perspective

Three simple exercises will help you stay worry free.

1. Feed your mind positive thoughts.

> Finally, brethren, whatever is true, whatever is honorable, whatever is right, whatever is pure, whatever is lovely, whatever is of good repute, if there is any excellence and if anything worthy of praise, let your mind dwell on these things.
>
> *Philippians 4:8*

No matter what you're dealing with or how bad things seem to be or why God may be permitting them, deliberately letting your mind dwell on positive, uplifting thoughts will enable you to survive. Literally. I frequently quote those words from Philippians 4:8 to myself. I say things like, "Okay, Chuck, it's time to let your mind dwell on better things." And then I go over the list and deliberately replace a worry with something far more honorable or pure or lovely, something worthy of praise. It never fails; the pressure I was feeling begins to fade and the peace I was missing begins to emerge.

2. Focus your attention on encouraging models.

> The things you have learned and received and heard and seen in me, practice these things.
>
> *Philippians 4:9a*

In the Philippians' case, Paul was their model. From his example, there were things to be learned and received and heard and seen. What a demonstration of encouragement he provided!

In your case and mine, it will help to focus our attention on someone we know and/or admire. That life, that encouraging model will give us a boost, a quick charge when our battery starts getting low.

3. Find "the God of Peace" in every circumstance.

> . . . and the God of peace shall be with you.
>
> *Philippians 4:9b*

This is the crowning achievement of recovering from anxiety addiction. Instead of living in the grip of fear, held captive by the chains of tension and dread, when we release our preoccupation with worry, we find God's hand at work on our behalf. He, our "God of peace," comes to our aid, changing people, relieving tension, altering difficult circumstances. The more you practice giving your mental burdens to the Lord, the more exciting it gets to see how God will handle the things that are impossible for you to do anything about. And as a result—you guessed it—you will begin to laugh again.

A PRINCIPLE . . . A PARROT

What is it, in the final analysis, that makes worry such an enemy of joy? Why does anxiety addiction take such a devastating toll on us? I have been thinking about that for months, and I believe I have the answer, which we might call a principle. At first it may seem simplistic, but this *is* the crux of the problem. This is exactly why anxiety holds us in such bondage.

WORRY FORCES US TO FOCUS
ON THE WRONG THINGS

Instead of essentials, we worry about nonessentials. Rather than looking at the known blessings that God provides today—so abundantly, so consistently—we worry about the unknown and uncertain events of tomorrow. Invariably, when we focus on the wrong things, we miss the main thing that life is all about.

That fact is vividly illustrated by one of my favorite stories. After more than forty years of marriage, this woman's husband suddenly died. For several months she sat alone in her house with the shades pulled and the door locked. Finally she decided she needed to do something about her situation. The loneliness was killing her.

She remembered that her husband had a friend who owned a nice pet store—a pet might be good company. So she dropped in one afternoon to look over the selection. She looked at dogs, cats, goldfish—even snakes! Nothing seemed quite right. She told the store owner she wanted a pet that could be a real companion—"almost like another human being in the house."

Suddenly he thought of one of his prized parrots. He showed her the colorful bird.

"Does it talk?"

"Absolutely . . . a real chatterbox. Everybody who comes in the store is astounded by this parrot's friendly disposition and wide vocabulary. That's why it's so expensive."

"Sold!" She bought the expensive parrot and hauled it home in a large, elegant cage. At last she had a companion she could talk to, who could answer back. Perfect!

But there was a problem. A full week passed without the bird's saying one word. Beginning to worry, she dropped by the pet shop.

"How's the parrot doing? Quite a talker, huh?"

"Not one word. I haven't been able to get a sound out of that bird. I'm worried!"

"Well, did you buy a *mirror* when you got the parrot and the cage last week?"

"Mirror? No. There's no mirror in the cage."

"That's your problem. A parrot needs a mirror. It's funny, but while looking at itself, a parrot starts to feel comfortable. In no time it will begin to talk." So she bought the mirror and put it into the cage.

Time passed, still nothing. Each day the woman talked to the bird, but not a peep came out of its beak. For hours on end she would talk as the parrot stared in silence. Another week passed without a word. By now she was really getting worried.

"The parrot isn't talking," she told the pet store owner. "I'm worried. All that money, the mirror—and still nothing."

"Say, did you buy a *ladder* when you got the cage?"

"A ladder? No. I didn't know it needed a ladder. Will that make it talk?"

"Works like a charm. The parrot will look in the mirror and get a little exercise, climbing up and down this ladder several times. Before long you won't believe what you hear. Trust me, you need the ladder."

She bought the ladder and put it into the cage next to the mirror . . . and waited. And waited. Another seven, eight days, still nothing. By now her worry was approaching the panic stage. "Why doesn't it talk?" That was all she could think about. She returned to the store in tears . . . with the same complaint.

"Did you buy a *swing?*"

"A swing! No. I have the cage, a mirror, and a ladder—I thought I had everything. I had no idea I needed a swing."

"Ya gotta have a swing. A parrot needs to feel completely at home. It glances in the mirror, takes a stroll up and down the ladder, and before long it's on the swing enjoying itself—and bingo! I've found that parrots usually talk when they are perched on a swing."

The woman bought the swing. She attached it to the top of the cage near the ladder and coaxed the parrot up the ladder and onto the swing. Still, absolute silence. For another ten days not one sound came from the cage.

Suddenly she came bursting into the pet store, really steaming. The owner met her at the counter.

"Hey, how's the parrot? I'll bet—"

"It died! My expensive bird is dead in the bottom of the cage."

"Well, I can't believe that. I'm just shocked. Did it ever say anything at all?"

"Yes, as a matter of fact, it did. As it lay there taking its last few breaths, it said very faintly, 'Don't they have any *food* down at that store?'"

There is no greater waste of our time and no greater deterrent to our joy than worry. By turning our attention to the wrong things, worry leads us to live our lives for the wrong reasons . . . and God is grieved. As I mentioned earlier in the book, God gives to His beloved even in our sleep. As we rejoice, relax, and rest, He relieves, renews, and restores.

A weary Christian lay awake one night trying to hold the world together by his worrying. Then he heard the Lord gently say to him, "Now you go to sleep, Jim; I'll sit up."[5]

13

*Don't Forget to
Have Fun As
You Grow Up*

I LIKE THE QUESTION ONCE ASKED by Satchel Paige, that venerable alumnus of baseball: "How old would you be if you didn't know how old you were?" An honest answer to that question depends on an honest admission of one's attitude. It has nothing to do with one's age. As someone young at heart has written:

> Remember, old folks are worth a fortune—silver in their hair, gold in their teeth, stones in their kidneys, lead in their feet, and gas in their stomachs.
>
> I have become a little older since I saw you last, and a few changes have come into my life since then. Frankly, I have become quite a frivolous old gal. I am seeing five gentlemen every day.
>
> As soon as I wake up, Will Power helps me get out of bed. Then I go to see John. Then Charlie Horse comes along, and when he is here he takes a lot of my time and attention. When he leaves Arthur Ritis shows up and stays the rest of the day. He doesn't like to stay in one place very long, so he takes me from joint to joint. After such a busy day I'm really tired and glad to go to bed with Ben Gay. What a life!
>
> P.S. The preacher came to call the other day. He said at my age I should be thinking about the hereafter. I told him, "Oh, I do all the time. No matter where I am—in the parlor, upstairs, in the kitchen, or down in the basement—I ask myself what am I here after?"[1]

The longer I live the more I become convinced that our major battle in life is not with age but with maturity. All of us are involuntary victims of the former. There is no choice involved in growing older. Our challenge is the choice of whether or not to grow up. It was Jesus who asked, "Who of you by worrying can add one inch to your height. . . or subtract one day from your age?" (Matt. 6:25–31). In other words, don't waste your time worrying about how old you are getting. Age is a matter of fact. Maturity, on the other hand, is a matter of choice.

You may be thinking, *Well, Chuck, that is all well and good, but you can't teach an old dog new tricks.* To which I respond with two reminders:

1. I am not writing to "old dogs." You are a person who has the capacity to think and to decide. Furthermore, if you are a Christian, you have the power of Christ within you, which means sufficient inner dynamic to effect incredible changes. If you are not a Christian, there is no time like the present to take care of that.

2. I am not teaching "tricks." The things you are reading are attainable and meaningful techniques that, when applied, can help you break old habits and form new ones. Admittedly the process of change may not come easy, but many have done it and you can too. The real question is not, "Am I able?" but, "Am I willing?"

Our becoming more mature is toward the top of the list on God's agenda for us. Repeatedly He mentions it in His Book:

> As a result, we are no longer to be children, tossed here and there by waves, and carried about by every wind of doctrine, by the trickery of men, by craftiness in deceitful scheming; but speaking the truth in love, we are to grow up in all aspects into Him, who is the head, even Christ.
>
> *Ephesians 4:14–15*

> Therefore, putting aside all malice and all guile and hypocrisy and envy and all slander, like newborn babes, long for the pure milk of the word, that by it you may grow in respect to salvation.
>
> *1 Peter 2:1–2*

> But solid food is for the mature, who because of practice have their senses trained to discern good and evil. Therefore leaving the elementary teaching about the Christ, let us press on to maturity, not laying again a foundation of repentance from dead works and of faith toward God.
>
> *Hebrews 5:14—6:1*

You and I are growing older. That's automatic. But that does not necessarily mean we are growing up. How important it is that we do so! And it will not happen unless we get control of our attitude, which turns us in the right direction. Let me urge you not to feed your mind with thoughts like: *I'm too far gone to change;* or, *Having been through all the things I've been through, there is no way I can alter my attitude.* Wrong! It is childish to play in the traffic of fear or let the hobgoblins of habit impede our progress. No one can win a race by continually looking back at where he or she has been. That will only demoralize, immobilize, and ultimately paralyze. God is for us. God's goal is that we move toward maturity, all our past failures and faults and hangups notwithstanding. I have seen many adults who thought they couldn't change begin to change. So I'm no longer willing to sit back and let anyone stay riveted to yesterday, thinking, *Woe is me.* Some of the most sweeping changes in my own life have occurred in my adult years. If it can happen in me, there is an enormous amount of hope for you. Attitudes can soar even if our circumstances lag and our past record sags.

God's specialty is bringing renewal to our strength, not reminders of our weakness. Take it by faith, He is well aware of your weaknesses; He just sovereignly chooses not to stop there. They become the platform upon which He does His best work. Cheer up! There is great hope. You won't be the first He helped from puberty to maturity.

THAT ELUSIVE QUALITY CALLED MATURITY

If maturity is all that important, we need to understand it better. The clearer it is in our minds, the easier it will be to get a focus on the target.

Exactly What Is It?

To be mature is to be fully developed, complete, and "grown up." Becoming mature is a process of consistently moving toward emotional and spiritual adulthood. In that process we leave childish and adolescent habits and adopt a lifestyle where we are fully responsible for our own decisions, motives, actions, and consequences. I heard someone say recently that maturity is developed and discerning competence as to how to live appropriately and to change rightly. In a word, it is *stability*. We never "arrive." We are always in the process of moving toward that objective. I have also observed that when maturity is taking place, balance replaces extremes and a seasoned confidence replaces uneasy feelings of insecurity. Good choices replace wrong ones.

How Is It Expressed?

Several things come to mind when I think of how all this works its way out. Marks of maturity are emerging—

- When our concern for others outweighs our concern for ourselves

- When we detect the presence of evil or danger before it is obvious

- When we have wisdom and understanding as well as knowledge

- When we have more than high ideals but also the discipline to carry them out

- When our emotions are tempered by responsibility and thoroughness

- When our awareness of needs is matched by our compassion and involvement

- When we not only understand a task but also have the fortitude to stay at it until it is done

- When we have a willingness to change, once we are convinced that correction is in order

- When we have the ability to grow spiritually by an independent intake of God's Word

One person summarized it in these words:

> Maturity is the ability to do a job whether you are supervised or not; finish a job once it's started; carry money without spending it. And last, but not least, the ability to bear an injustice without wanting to get even.[2]

TWO SIDES OF THE SAME QUALITY

Most folks I know would agree that those things describe where we would like to be personally. When we think of growing up, that is what we have in mind. Once we are there, who wouldn't have reason to rejoice? But the fact is, if we maintain the right attitude we are able to rejoice while in the process of getting there. That is what is so exciting about Paul's words to his friends in Philippi. Throughout the letter he has continued to emphasize and encourage outrageous joy in spite of difficult circumstances, because of Christ. In fact, that is exactly where this next section begins.

> But I rejoiced in the Lord greatly, that now at last you have revived your concern for me; indeed, you were concerned before, but you lacked opportunity.
>
> *Philippians 4:10*

Who is saying this? Some young turk who has just turned the deal on his first million? A superstar who recently signed an unbelievable contract? Some guy in his twenties about to set sail on a magnificent adventure? Not on your life. Would you believe, a sixty-plus-year-old Jew chained to a Roman guard under house arrest, not knowing if tomorrow he will be killed, brought to court, or set free? Though getting up in years, he is rejoicing. Though without the comforts of home and the privileges of privacy, he is happy. Though he doesn't have a clue regarding his future, he is smiling at life. Though he is set aside, forced to stay in one place, completely removed from the excitement of a broader minisry, he is still rejoicing, still laughing. No matter what happened to him, Paul refused to be caught in the grip of pessimism.

Maturity of Paul

We are able to get a pretty good glimpse here of the man who truly practiced what he preached. I find in this section of his letter at least four characteristics of maturity in Paul's life.

1. He is affirming.

> But I rejoiced in the Lord greatly, that now at last you have revived your concern for me; indeed, you were concerned before, but you lacked opportunity.
>
> *Philippians 4:10*

The words could sound mysterious if you didn't understand that behind them is the financial support of the Philippians. When he writes that they had revived their concern for him, Paul means that they had sent another contribution to help him press on. Don't miss a little detail here. When he says, "You were concerned before, but you lacked opportunity," he means they had wanted to send an offering to him earlier, but they either didn't know where he was or they had no way to get it to him. Normally it is the other way around! We have an opportunity to send our support, but we lack concern.

I am impressed with Paul's affirmation of his friends. This is a thank-you letter . . . a "receipt letter," if you will. The implication is so thoughtful: Even when I didn't hear from you, you were concerned for me. Paul thought better of others, not less. He upheld their intentions. Even when he didn't hear from his friends, he did not doubt that they cared.

We appreciate what people do. We affirm who they are. When we say thank you to someone who completes a task, we are expressing our appreciation. But when we acknowledge and express our gratitude for what others are—in character, in motive, in heart—we are affirming them personally. A mark of maturity is the ability to affirm, not just appreciate. How easy to see people (especially family members and fellow workers at our place of employment) as doers of tasks, but a task-oriented mentality is incomplete. And as important as appreciation for a job well done may be, it too is incomplete. People are not human tools appointed to accomplish a set of tasks, but human beings with souls, with feelings. How essential it is to recognize and affirm the unseen, hidden qualities that make an individual a person of worth and dignity. The best leaders (like Paul) appreciate and affirm.

Max DePree is chairman and chief executive officer of Herman Miller, Inc., the furniture maker that was named one of *Fortune* magazine's ten best managed and most innovative companies. It was also chosen as one of the hundred best companies to work for in America. In his book, *Leadership Is an Art,* DePree touches on the importance of understanding and acknowledging the diversity of people's inner gifts and unseen talents. What he describes has to do with affirmation.

My father is ninety-six years old. He is the founder of Herman Miller, and much of the value system and impounded energy of the company, a legacy still drawn on today, is a part of his contribution. In the furniture industry of the 1920s the machines of most factories were not run by electric motors, but by pulleys from a central drive shaft. The central drive shaft was run by the steam engine. The steam engine got its steam from the boiler. The boiler, in our case, got its fuel from the sawdust and other waste coming out of the machine room—a beautiful cycle.

The millwright was the person who oversaw that cycle and on whom the entire activity of the operation depended. He was a key person.

One day the millwright died.

My father, being a young manager at the time, did not particularly know what he should do when a key person died, but thought he ought to go visit the family. He went to the house and was invited to join the family in the living room. There was some awkward conversation—the kind with which many of us are familiar.

The widow asked my father if it would be all right if she read aloud some poetry. Naturally, he agreed. She went into another room, came back with a bound book, and for many minutes read selected pieces of beautiful poetry. When she finished, my father commented on how beautiful the poetry was and asked who wrote it. She replied that her husband, the millwright, was the poet.

It is now nearly sixty years since the millwright died, and my father and many of us at Herman Miller continue to wonder: Was he a poet who did millwright's work, or was he a millwright who wrote poetry?

In our effort to understand corporate life, what is it we should learn from this story? In addition to all of the ratios and goals and parameters and bottom lines, it is fundamental that leaders endorse a concept of persons. This begins with an understanding of the diversity of people's gifts and talents and skills.[3]

2. He is contented.

Not that I speak from want; for I have learned to be content in whatever circumstances I am.

Philippians 4:11

As valuable as affirmation may be, maturity is never more obvious than when an individual evidences contentment. And no one was a better model than Paul, who "learned to be content," regardless of his situation. To him it made no difference whether he was freed or bound to a soldier . . . whether the day was hot and humid or bleak and frigid . . . whether the Philippians sent a gift or failed to make contact. How wonderfully refreshing. How incredibly mature!

Some people are thermometers. They merely *register* what is around them. If the situation is tight and pressurized, they register tension and irritability. If it's stormy, they register worry and fear. If it's calm, quiet, and comfortable, they register relaxation and peacefulness.

Others, however, are thermostats. They *regulate* the atmosphere. They are the mature change-agents who never let the situation dictate to them.

217

You are probably thinking, *I wish I had that "contentment gift."* Wait. It isn't a gift. It is a learned trait. Paul admits that he has developed the ability to accept and to adapt. Remember? He wrote, "I have *learned* to be content."

That reminds me of the comment we heard from several men who had been prisoners of war during the Vietnam War and survived the horrors of Hanoi. A number of those brave men said the same thing: "We learned after a few hours what it took to survive, and we just adapted to that." They didn't whine and complain because they had been captured. They didn't eat their hearts out because the conditions were miserable and the food was terrible. They chose to adapt.

Interestingly, the Greek term translated "content" does not mean, "I don't care what happens—I'll remain indifferent, numb." No, this unusual term suggests "self-sufficient," and in the context of this letter it means being at peace in Christ's sufficiency. How could Paul adapt and endure? What was it that relieved the tension and allowed him to be so relaxed within? He was convinced that Christ was in the midst of his every day, pouring His power into him. When we believe that, *anything* is bearable. *Nothing* is out of control. When we genuinely have that attitude, laughter comes easily, naturally.

3. He is flexible.

> I know how to get along with humble means, and I also know how to live in prosperity; in any and every circumstance I have learned the secret of being filled and going hungry, both of having abundance and suffering need.

> *Philippians 4:12*

What an enviable list. Three strong contrasts illustrate the man's ability to adapt.

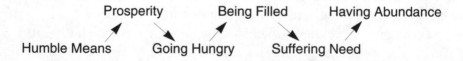

In the yo-yo of life, it is essential to flex. Paul wasn't ticked off because he was on the street, sleeping under a bridge with a growling stomach. Neither was he uneasy in the penthouse, enjoying delicious meals in abundance. When without, he didn't grumble. And when blessed he didn't act unworthy and ashamed. Mature men and women can handle both without disturbing their spiritual or emotional equilibrium.

For some strange reason, most Christians I know struggle more with having an abundance than with suffering great need. Maybe that explains the tendency among Christians to judge and criticize other believers who have wealth and lovely possessions, even though they earned it honestly and hold it all loosely. What graceless immaturity! For some weird reason we would rather brag about how little we have than thankfully relax in a context of God-given prosperity. Am I promoting some kind of "prosperity" gospel? In no way; I think such teaching is heresy. But my concern here is that we be just as willing "to rejoice with those who rejoice" as we are "to weep with those who weep" (Rom. 12:15). When I meet those who cannot do both with equal passion and support, I realize that the problem is immaturity. What concerns me the most is the lack of interest in learning to change in that area.

4. He is confident.

> I can do all things through Him who strengthens me.
> *Philippians 4:13*

I mentioned earlier that Paul demonstrated self-sufficiency in his contentment. Here is the statement I referred to when I said that he was sufficient in Christ's sufficiency. The Living Bible puts it this way:

> For I can do everything God asks me to with the help of Christ who gives me the strength and power.

No statement in Scripture speaks more clearly of the indwelling Christ. Our Savior not only *lives* within each of His people, He also *pours His power* into us. And that alone is enough to make us confident.

Consider again Paul's statement. Whatever we may substitute for "Christ" fails to fit the statement. Let's try several.

"I can do all things through *drugs*." No.

"I can do all things through *education*." No.

"I can do all things through *money*." No.

"I can do all things through *success*." No.

"I can do all things through *friends*." No.

"I can do all things through *positive thinking*." No.

"I can do all things through *political office*." No.

Nothing else fits . . . only Christ. Why? Because nothing and no one else is able to empower us and provide the strength we need. Because the Christian has the Lord Himself dwelling within, the potential for inner strength (i.e., confidence) is unlimited. This explains why those who gave their lives for whatever righteous cause down through the ages did so with such courage. Often they were physically weak individuals, small in stature, but they refused to back down. Only the indwelling, empowering Christ can give someone that much confidence. It is almost as if He gives us a feeling of victorious invincibility. That kind of mature confidence enables us to laugh in the face of resistance.

Maturity of the Philippians

We found four qualities of maturity in Paul.

- Affirming others
- Contented, regardless
- Flexible, whatever the situation
- Confident through Christ

I find it interesting that his Christian friends in Philippi, according to what he wrote of them, also demonstrated maturity. I find at least three characteristics in their lives.

1. Personal compassion.

> Nevertheless, you have done well to share with me in my affliction. And you yourselves also know, Philippians, that at the first preaching of the gospel, after I departed from Macedonia, no church shared with me in the matter of giving and receiving but you alone.
>
> *Philippians 4:14–15*

Paul had numerous needs as he traveled on his missionary journeys. He endured hardship and disappointments, heartaches and afflictions.

Through it all, the Philippians lent their support. In fact, no other church demonstrated such personal compassion—a mark of maturity. They never second-guessed the apostle in his decision to move on; they supported him. They neither judged him when things went well nor complained when times were hard and he had no fruit to show for his labor; they supported him. They felt pain when he hurt, they prayed for him when he was unable to stay in touch, and they sent friends to comfort him when he was in prison. What a church! No wonder he felt such affection for them.

  2. Financial generosity.

> For even in Thessalonica you sent a gift more than once for my needs. Not that I seek the gift itself, but I seek for the profit which increases to your account.

> *Philippians 4:16–17*

  There is perhaps no finer evidence of maturity than financial generosity. When people graciously and liberally release their treasure to the cause of Christ, it is a sign that they are growing up. The people of Philippi were models of this—"even in Thessalonica." That was a wealthier city than Philippi. Yet even when Paul was there, the Philippians kept right on giving.

  By the way, don't rush over that second sentence ("Not that I seek . . .") too quickly. Paul wasn't interested in getting their money; rather, he was seeking their best interest. Am I saying he didn't need their financial contributions? On the contrary. He probably could not have survived without them.

  We need a whole new mentality when it comes to thinking clearly about money. The greed of this era has caused the subject of money to be tainted and misunderstood. Money, however, is not evil. It is immature to think it is. While it can be abused and can become the cause for all sorts of evil (1 Tim. 6:10), how one handles this medium of exchange is often a good barometer of one's spiritual and emotional growth. Very few things get accomplished in the realm of ministry without the presence of generous financial support from God's choice servants. Let's face it, money and ministry often flow together. There is nothing unspiritual about admitting the need for money in our lives. To quote the great Sophie Tucker:

From birth to eighteen, a girl needs good parents.
From eighteen to thirty-five, she needs good looks.
From thirty-five to fifty-five, she needs a good
    personality.
From fifty-five on, she needs cash.[4]

Paul's need was for cash, no question about it. Because his friends were mature, they responded generously.

3. Sacrificial Commitment.

> But I have received everything in full, and have an abundance; I am amply supplied, having received from Epaphroditus what you have sent, a fragrant aroma, an acceptable sacrifice, well-pleasing to God.
>
> *Philippians 4:18*

As Paul took stock of his situation, he realized he couldn't have been better taken care of. As he put it, he was "amply supplied." He had more than enough. Thanks to the sacrificial commitment of the Philippians, his needs were wonderfully met. And isn't that the way it is supposed to be? As the gift is given, prompted by the Spirit of God, it comes as "a fragrant aroma," giving God great delight.

It is as if Paul's heart suddenly bursts forth with gratitude as he writes this splendid promise to his friends:

> And my God shall supply all your needs according to His riches in glory in Christ Jesus.
>
> *Philippians 4:19*

When God is in our hearts of compassion, prompting us to get involved in helping others . . . when He is in our acts of generosity, honoring our support of those engaged in ministry . . . and when He is in our strong commitment, using our sacrifices to bless other lives, He does not forget us in our need. It is all so beautiful, so simple, so right. It is enough to make every one of us *laugh out loud!*

But there is a flip side to all this where something meant to be simple and beautiful can become slick and ugly. The whole subject of finances and fund raising and remaining pure, humble, and grateful in the handling of money is a heavy weight hanging on the thin wires of integrity and accountability. Because a few ministries, rare negative examples, have made the news over the misuse of funds, some would discredit all ministries who need the support of God's people. That is both unfortunate and unfair. All physicians are not viewed with suspicion because a few have been guilty of malpractice. God honors the sacrificial commitment of His people and promises His blessing on those who give that His work might go on.

It is as if Paul is summing up his thoughts with the final verse:

My God . . .

> your needs . . .

> > His riches. . . .

When those three ingredients blend together under the control of the Holy Spirit, it is *something* to behold!

Before we bring this chapter to a close, I want to address the importance of earning the respect of those who continue to support a ministry. As Paul maintained a life of trust and faith and quiet confidence in God, the people in Philippi did not hesitate to stand with him financially. Though he occasionally enjoyed times of abundance and prosperity, Paul never became enamored by his success. He assumed nothing and continued to walk humbly with his God. He refused to believe his own press clippings or lose sight of God's hand in it all.

When the PTL scandal grabbed the attention of the national media, so many in the church, including myself, watched in embarrassed disbelief. As one disgraceful act after another became public knowledge, our disbelief turned to shock and shame. All of us wondered how such things could have happened in a ministry. Some of the answers were provided in an interview *Christianity Today* did with Richard Dortch, who was on staff as PTL grew in popularity. Of special interest to me was his description of how the managers of that organization came to define success:

> It is all tied to how many stations we have on our network or how big our building is. It is so easy to lose control, to compromise without recognizing it. At PTL, there was not time taken for prayer or family because the show had to go on. We were so caught up in God's work that we forgot about God.[5]

With unusual candor, Mr. Dortch also mentioned the incredible impact of television on the one up-front under the bright lights, always before an applauding audience:

A television camera can change a preacher quicker than anything else. Those who sit on the sidelines can notice the changes in people once they get in front of a camera. It turns a good man into a potentate. It is so easy to get swept away by popularity: Everybody loves you, cars are waiting for you, and you go to the head of the line. That is the devastation of the camera. It has made us less than what God has wanted us to become.[6]

Mr. Dortch's words sound forth another grim reminder that maturity, integrity, and accountability must remain present if we hope to know the blessing of God. People's support is a sacred trust, never to be taken lightly.

MAKING MATURITY A PERSONAL MATTER

How can these truths get lifted from the printed page and transferred to our lives? What's necessary if we hope to break the selfish syndrome and accelerate our growth toward maturity? Let me leave you three bones to chew on:

1. Look within . . . and release. What is it down inside you that is stunting your growth? When you probe around and find something you are hanging onto too tightly, deliberately let go. Yes, you can. You just read it from Paul's pen. You "can do all things through Christ." Let Him help you pry your fingers loose. Inner joy begins when you have "no other gods before you."

2. Look around . . . and respond. Don't wait for someone else. Act on your own, spontaneously. The Philippians saw Paul in his need and they responded . . . again and again. Even though other churches did not follow their example, those folks from Philippi saw the need and responded. Is there some need you can help meet? Risk responding.

3. Look up . . . and rejoice. You are the recipient of His riches—enjoy them! Realize anew all He has done for you; then rejoice in the pleasure of getting involved with others. Among the happiest people are those who voluntarily serve others to the glory of God. Some of the saddest are people who have ceased all contact with those in need.

A comment from Jeanne Hendricks' fine volume, *Afternoon*, has helped me remember this:

Living is not a spectator sport. No one, at any price, is privileged to sit in the stands and watch the action from a distance. Being born means

224

being a participant in the arena of life, where opposition is fierce and winning comes only to those who exert every ounce of energy.[7]

Laughter is definitely connected to staying involved with people. Stay involved! You will never regret it. Furthermore, it will help you grow up as you find yourself growing old. And the more involved you remain, the less concern you will have for how old you are.

By the way, how old *would* you be if you didn't know how old you were?

14

A Joyful, Grace-Filled Good-bye

THIS HAS BEEN THE MOST ENJOYABLE BOOK I have written. The chapters have flowed together (an author's dream!), and the theme of outrageous joy and laughter has lifted my own spirits immensely. I am convinced the Lord knew I needed a dose of my own medicine. With all the heaviness and "bad-news blues" I have had to wade through lately, I was ready for a lighthearted shot in the arm. It worked. I hope it has for you too.

All that prompts a confession: I get weary of believers who live their entire lives with such long faces and nothing but woe-is-me words pouring from their mouths. I realize that life isn't one continually blooming rose garden (mine certainly isn't), but surely it is more than Lamentations Lane. I look at some who claim to be "happy within," and I wonder if maybe they were baptized in freshly squeezed lemon juice. When did we buy into that nonsense? Each time I look up and see Dr. Dryasdust and his wife Grimly making their way toward me, I find myself wanting to run and hide or, better, be raptured out!

Reminds me of a cartoon every mother of small children will appreciate. A little freckled-faced boy, five or six years old, is standing in his pajamas outside his parents' bedroom door—which is shut *and locked.* He looks like the type who would keep six or seven healthy adults jumping. The bottom of his pajamas is unsnapped, his diaper is bagging and soaked, his teddy bear has had its nose torn off and one button-eye is dangling, the other missing. He is staring at a sign, hanging from the doorknob, on which his mom has scribbled

CLOSED FOR BUSINESS!
MOTHERHOOD OUT OF ORDER

There are days I'm tempted to do the same on my study door. Only my sign would read something like:

I'VE HEARD ENOUGH!
MINISTER OUT OT ORDER
GONE RIDIN' ON MY HARLEY
BE BACK IN TWO DAYS—MAYBE

There are days a guy like me (and perhaps you can identify) starts running out of ideas on how to help folks fix their messed-up lives. Sometimes the more I try, the worse the mess. Ever had that happen? Then you understand. But maybe not as well as a fellow named R. D. Jones. "Dear Abby" mentioned him in one of her newspaper columns several months ago. It had to do with a typographical error in the classified section of a small-town newspaper and the subsequent disastrous attempts to correct it. Things went from bad to worse to *horrible*.

Monday: FOR SALE—R. D. Jones has one sewing machine for sale. Phone 948–0707 after 7 p.m. and ask for Mrs. Kelly who lives with him cheap.

Tuesday: NOTICE—We regret having erred in R. D. Jones' ad yesterday. It should have read: One sewing machine for sale. Cheap. Phone 948–0707 and ask for Mrs. Kelly who lives with him after 7 p.m.

Wednesday: NOTICE—R. D. Jones has informed us that he has received several annoying telephone calls because of the error we made in his classified ad yesterday. His ad stands corrected as follows: FOR SALE—R. D. Jones has one sewing machine for sale. Cheap. Phone 948–0707 p.m. and ask for Mrs. Kelly who loves with him.

Thursday: NOTICE—I, R. D. Jones, have NO sewing machine for sale. I SMASHED IT. Don't call 948–0707, as the telephone has been disconnected. I have not been carrying on with Mrs. Kelly. Until yesterday she was my housekeeper, but she quit.[1]

I suggest that R. D. Jones pick up a copy of my book on Friday and start reading right away. And Mrs. Kelly should spend the whole weekend in it, nonstop.

At times like that we need to find relief from life's blistering winds of disappointment and discouragement. For me, nothing works better than a break in the schedule where hearty laughter and a whole change of pace takes my mind off the demands and deadlines. And of all the books in the Bible that help bring a fresh perspective, Philippians tops the list. Again and again it reminds us that we can choose joy regardless of our circumstances, our financial status, our occupation, our past failures, or our current distresses. Thank goodness, things don't have to be perfect or nearly perfect in order for us to focus on the bright side of life.

WHERE HAVE WE BEEN?

Since we have come to the last few words Paul wrote his friends at Philippi, this is a good time to do a little review of where we have been. Threaded through the fabric of this delightful letter has been an overriding theme of joy and rejoicing.

- In chapter 1 of the letter we found *joy in living.* Can you remember? It was there the Apostle of Grace communicated, "For me to live is Christ" (1:21). As long as Christ is central in my life, nothing can steal that joy He brings.

- In chapter 2 of Philippians we discovered there is *joy in serving.* And from whom do we learn this? Again, Christ is the model. With an attitude of submission and acceptance, He left the splendor of heaven in order to come and serve others on earth.

- In chapter 3 *joy in submitting* was the prominent message. Christ, according to that chapter, is our goal. Paul lists all his accomplishments and human effort then admits that, compared to Christ, those things he "counted as loss." Zero. Compared to Christ's righteousness, human effort is nothing more than cotton candy.

- In chapter 4 we learned there is *joy in resting.* Why? Because Jesus Christ is our cause for contentment. We can rest in Him, and as we do, He pours His power into us. When He does that our confidence is re-ignited and restored.

This little letter, the most upbeat of all those Paul wrote, never fails to silence the naysayers and lift our spirits. Surrounded by so many who are down in the mouth, convinced we are headed for doom (with statistics to prove it), we need the reminder that Christ is still triumphant. Our circumstances may be challenging, but God is not wringing His hands, wondering how He is going to work things out. That kind of negative reasoning deserves one of my favorite Greek words in response: *Hogwash*.

I love the way G. Campbell Morgan addresses all this:

> I have no sympathy with people who tell us today that these are the darkest days the world has ever seen. The days in which we live are appalling, but they do not compare with conditions in the world when Jesus came into it. Historians talk of the *Pax Romana* and make much of the fact that there was peace everywhere, the Roman peace. Do not forget that the Roman peace was the result of the fact that the world had been bludgeoned brutally into submission to one central power. . . .
>
> Notwithstanding the prevailing conditions, the dominant note of these Letters, revealing the experience of the Church, is a note of triumph. The dire and dread facts and conditions are never lost sight of—indeed, they are there all the way through. The people are seen going out and facing these facts—and suffering because of these facts—but we never see them depressed and cast down, we never see them suffering from pessimistic fever. They are always triumphant. That is the glory of Christianity. If ever I am tempted to think that religion is almost dead today, it is when I listen to the wailing of some Christian people: "Everything is wrong," or "Everything is going wrong." Oh, be quiet! Think again, look again, judge not by the circumstances of the passing hour but by the infinite things of our Gospel and our God. And that is exactly what these people did.[2]

I love his spunk when encountering the grumblers and doomsayers: "Oh, be quiet!"

How Do We Proceed?

Let's take a look at Paul's closing comments. Read his words slowly, deliberately pausing at the important terms he uses:

> And my God shall supply all your needs according to His riches in glory in Christ Jesus. Now to our God and Father be the glory forever and ever. Amen.

Greet every saint in Christ Jesus. The brethren who are with me greet you. All the saints greet you, especially those of Caesar's household.

The grace of the Lord Jesus Christ be with your spirit.

Philippians 4:19–23

Unlike the fanfares of a grand symphonic cadence, Paul says farewell in an understated manner. I find about four staccatolike statements.

First, *he writes of the glory of the Lord's plan.* Hidden in the throne room of God's celestial existence are "riches in glory." He blesses us and He provides for us according to those riches. He draws upon that infinite supply base as He meets our every need. And when He does, He gets the corresponding glory . . . forever. Look how Paul puts it:

And it is he who will supply all your needs from his riches in glory, because of what Christ Jesus has done for us. Now unto God our Father be glory forever and ever. Amen.

Philippians 4:19–20 TLB

God gives from His "riches in glory," and, in turn, He receives the glory. We would say He gets the credit. Need a few examples?

- When your boss walks in and congratulates you—you are being promoted—God gets the glory. Of course you feel good about it and you worked hard for it, but the credit is God's.

- An illness has plagued you for weeks, perhaps months. While you prayed and sought qualified medical attention during that time, little changed. To your own amazement, God steps in and solves the dilemma. Who can ever explain the healing that He miraculously performed? We cannot explain it, but we *can* give Him the glory. And because we can, we *must*.

- One of your children has been a special challenge. Virtually since birth, he (or she) has been difficult. About the time you are ready to throw up your hands and say, "I've had it!" the Lord steps in and "supplies all your need according to His riches in glory," and your almost-grown challenge suddenly changes and begins to model manners, responsibility,

233

and courtesy. As a result, God gets the glory . . . as you begin to laugh again.

How happy are those to whom God demonstrates His glory.
Second, *he mentions the greeting of the saints.*

> Greet every saint in Christ Jesus. The brethren who are with me greet you. All the saints greet you, especially those of Caesar's household.
>
> *Philippians 4:21–22*

As you can imagine, those words have spurred imaginations for centuries. The intriguing part is Paul's reference to "Caesar's household." Could he have in mind the emperor's wife and children? Would it be broader than that and encompass the in-laws and distant relatives? Does Paul mean the *literal* household?

The most reliable scholarship suggests that it is a reference to an incredibly large body of people in Italy and the surrounding provinces, slaves and free citizens alike . . . members of the elite Imperial Guard that waited on Caesar, doing his special work. And we should not forget the network of executives and administrators, secretaries and courtiers in and about Caesar's royal palace.

If you find this fascinating, as I certainly do, the following quotations will tweak your interest further.

J. B. Lightfoot writes:

> It has been assumed that this phrase must designate persons of high rank and position, powerful minions of the court, great officers of state, or even blood relations to the Emperor himself. . . . The 'domus' or 'familia Caesaris' . . . includes the whole of the imperial household, the meanest [lowest] slaves as well as the most powerful courtiers. . . . In Rome itself . . . the 'domus Augusta' must have formed no inconsiderable fraction of the whole population; but it comprised likewise all persons in the emperor's service, whether slaves or freemen, in Italy and even in the provinces.[3]

William Ramsey, in his fascinating classic, *St. Paul, the Traveller and the Roman Citizen,* adds this:

> The new movement made marked progress in the vast Imperial household. . . . The Imperial household was at the centre of affairs and

in most intimate relations with all parts of the Empire. . . . There can be no doubt that . . . Christianity effected an entrance into Caesar's household before Paul entered Rome; in all probability he is right also in thinking that all the slaves of Aristobulus (son of Herod the Great) and of Narcissus (Claudius's favourite freedman) had passed into the Imperial household, and that members of these two *familiae* are saluted as Christians by Paul (Rom. 16:10–16).[4]

One other, from Alfred Plummer of Trinity College at Oxford:

There were many Jews among the lower officials in Nero's household, and it was perhaps among them that the Gospel made its first converts.[5]

Legend has it that while Nero was out of town, his wife listened to the Christian message and turned her life over to Christ. When Nero returned and discovered she had been converted to Christ, his anger knew no bounds! Perhaps it was that which led to his rash decision to behead Paul.

The point I am making is that the remarkable spread of the gospel is enough to make all of us laugh out loud! Christ had invaded and infiltrated the very citadel of unbelief. Isn't that a great thought? In the very rooms where His name had been an unmentionable, Christ as Lord was now being openly discussed. And all of that was happening right under Nero's nose—yet he couldn't stop it!

Our minister of music at the church I serve, Howie Stevenson, and his wife, Marilyn, along with several friends from our church and many others from the United States, had the privilege of taking their talents to Moscow during the Russian Orthodox Easter in 1991. It was a vast gathering of Christians and non-Christians alike. The actual place of ministry was the Palace of Congress where the Supreme Soviet had met for years. You've seen the massive room on television, with the enormous oversize picture of Lenin hung before all in attendance. Except, in this case, Lenin's portrait was covered. And instead of communism's propaganda being proclaimed, Bill Bright, of Campus Crusade for Christ, preached the gospel. Howie, accompanied by his wife and two of my favorite musical artists, Stephen Nielson and Ovid Young, on dual pianos, led a large choir who presented the praises of Jesus Christ in the very stronghold of atheism.

The halls were filled with the majestic music of the Messiah, Jesus Christ, whose message of forgiveness and grace was announced by television to millions of viewers in the land of Russia . . . the very place where a few years ago you would be immediately arrested for merely mentioning the name of Jesus Christ.

On Sunday afternoon the group went into Red Square and distributed more than a hundred thousand pamphlets that conveyed the message of Christ, including Testaments and Bibles in the language of the people. (Actually they were warned against doing that too aggressively because they might be mobbed by people starving for more information about Christ.)

Isn't that great! They announced in music and spoken word that Jesus Christ is the Savior, the Lord, the risen Supreme One. We could say that Christ was proclaimed "even in Lenin's household." I must confess, when Howie reported on the marvelous success of their trip and everyone in our church applauded vigorously, I thought, *In your face, Lenin! Our God reigns.*

As I write this I am smiling. The thought of that triumphant message being publicly proclaimed in a once-forbidden region of our world is enough to make me laugh out loud. I cannot help but wonder if Paul, chained to that uniformed and armed guard in his little house in Rome, didn't smile with delight as he pictured the irresistible, life-changing movement of Christianity pushing its way into the least likely areas of Nero's domain. Yes, *our God reigns!*

Third, *Paul reaffirms the grace of the Savior.* We would expect this from him, wouldn't we? Grace had become the very theme of his life by now. Law had come by Moses, but grace came through Jesus Christ. It was grace that reached Paul en route to Damascus. It was grace that saved him as he realized all those accomplishments of his past were deeds done in the flesh. It became obvious to him that grace would be his message as he was used by God to minister to Gentiles and offer them the hope of sins forgiven and a home in heaven. And it was grace that assured him of his own eternal destiny. Any man whose life had been transformed so radically, so completely, because of God's matchless grace would naturally shout it from the housetop for the rest of his life.

As John Newton wrote with equal passion centuries later:

> Through many dangers, toils, and snares,
> I have already come;
> 'Tis grace hath brought me safe thus far,
> And grace will lead me home.[6]

I never sing that grand old hymn without thanking God anew that in spite of all those things He could have held against me, He accepted me, forgave me, included me in His family, and will some day receive me into glory. If that isn't enough to make us laugh again, I don't know what is.

What a magnificent letter Paul wrote from Rome to his friends far away in Philippi. I can imagine the gray-haired apostle reaching his manacled arm over to Epaphroditus, taking the stylus from his hand . . . and forming these closing words with his own fingers:

> **To our God and Father be the glory forever and ever. Greet every saint in Christ Jesus. . . . All the saints greet you, especially those of Caesar's household. . . . Grace . . . be with your spirit. Amen.**
>
> Paulos

And with that Paul rolled up the scroll, embraced his friend with a smile, and sent him on his way with letter in hand, having prayed for journey mercies. I can see Paul smiling as he waved a joyful, grace-filled good-bye to a man he would never see again on earth.

A Treasured Legacy

When I completed my own study of the letter to the Philippians, I experienced a nostalgic serendipity. As I was putting away my research materials along with pen and paper, an old book by F. B. Meyer, one of my favorite authors, caught my attention. It happened to be his work on Philippians, but I had not consulted it throughout my months of study.

Thinking there might be something in it to augment my study, I decided to pull it from the shelf and leaf through it before I went home for the day. I turned off the overhead light in my study, and, with only the light from my desk lamp, I leaned back in my old leather desk chair and opened Meyer's book.

To my unexpected delight, it was not the words of F. B. Meyer that spoke to me that evening, but the words of my mother. For as I began looking through it, I realized this book was one of the many volumes which had found their way from her library into mine after her death back in 1971. Little did she know when she wrote in it years before that her words would become a part of her legacy to me, her youngest. I sat very still as I took in the wonder.

In her own inimitable handwriting, my mother had made notes in the text and along the margins throughout the book. When I got to the end, I noticed she had penned these words on the inside of the back cover, "Finished reading this May 8, 1958."

I looked up in my dimly lit study and pondered, *1958.* My mind took me back to a tiny island in the South Pacific where I had spent many lonely months as a Marine. I recalled that it was *in May of 1958* that I had reached a crossroad in my own pilgrimage. In fact, I had entered the following words in my journal: "The Lord has convinced me that I am to be in His service. I will begin to make plans to prepare for a lifetime of ministry." Amazingly, it was in the same month of that very year that my mother had finished reading Meyer's book. As I looked back over the pages, I found one reference after another to her prayers for me as I was away . . . her concern for my spiritual welfare . . . her desire for God's best in my life. And occasionally she had inserted a clever quip or humorous comment.

Turning back to the front of the book, I found another interesting entry, also with a date. It read, "Chart of Philippians mailed to me by Charles when he was ministering in Massachusetts, 1966." As I glanced over the chart, another memory swept over me. I recalled putting that chart together and sending it to her during my years in New England. Once again I looked up and momentarily relived those years between 1958 and 1966. What a significant passage! All through that time, I now realize my mother had prayed for me and loved me and sought God's best for me.

Across the room in my study hangs an original oil painting with a light above it, shedding a golden glow down over the colorful canvas. The painting was my mother's gift to me some years after I entered the ministry. She had painted it. It is of a shepherd surrounded by a handful of sheep on a green hillside.

I had looked at this painting countless times before, but this time was unique. In the bottom right corner I looked at her name and the date . . . only days before she passed into the Lord's presence. Caught in that nostalgic time warp, I turned off my desk lamp and stared at the lighted painting. There I sat, twenty years after she had laid the brush aside, thanking God anew for my mother's prayers, my pilgrimage, and especially His presence. Faithfully, graciously, quietly He had led me and helped me and blessed me. I bowed my head and thanked Him for His sustaining grace . . . and I wept with gratitude.

Suddenly the shrill sound of the telephone broke the silence. My younger son, Chuck, was on the line wanting to tell me something funny that had happened. I quickly switched gears and enjoyed one of those delightful, lighthearted father-son moments. As we laughed loudly together, he urged me to hurry home.

Following his call I placed the F. B. Meyer book back on the shelf. As I was leaving my study, I paused beside the painting and thought of the significant role my parents had played in those formative years of my life . . . and how the torch had been passed on from them to Cynthia and me to do the same with our sons and daughters . . . and they, in turn, with theirs.

As I switched off the light above the painting, I smiled and said, "Good-bye, Mother." In the darkness of that room I could almost hear her voice answering me, "Good-bye, Charles. I love you, Son. I'm still praying for you. Keep walking with God . . . and don't forget to have some fun with your family tonight."

What a treasured legacy: devoted prayers, lasting love, hearty laughter. That's the way it ought to be.

Conclusion

God's sense of humor has intrigued me for years. What amazes me, however, is the number of people who don't think He has one. For the life of me, I can't figure out why they can't see it. He made you and me, didn't He? And what about all those funny-looking creatures that keep drawing us back to the zoo? If they aren't proof of our Creator's sense of humor, I don't know what is. Have you taken a close look at a wombat or a two-toed sloth, a giant anteater or a warthog lately? They're hilarious! Every time I look at a camel I chuckle, recalling the words of some wag who said it reminded him of a horse put together by a committee. I honestly wonder if God didn't laugh Himself as He dropped some of those creatures on our planet eons ago.

God's humor, unfortunately, does not occupy any significant place in serious works of theology. I know; I've been checking them for years and been disappointed. In my four intensive years of study in an excellent graduate school of theology, I don't recall one time that any prof addressed the subject of God's sense of humor. And in all my reading since then—thirty years of searching—seldom have I found anything more than a lighthearted throwaway line on the subject.

That's too bad. Because the impression we are left with is that our Lord is an all-too-serious Sovereign who has no room in His character for at least a few moments of fun. At best this frowning, uptight caricature suggests He is a heavenly representation of some venerable, earthly theologian—only older and wiser. Please!

Surely it is not blasphemous to think that laughter breaks out in heaven on special occasions. Why shouldn't it? There is every reason to believe that would happen in His infinite, holy presence, where all is well and no evil abides. After all, God sees everything that transpires in this human comedy of errors . . . He understands it all.

He must have smiled, for example, when Elijah mocked the false prophets on Mount Carmel, asking whether their gods had gone on a journey or fallen asleep or were *indisposed* (1 Kings 18:27)! And what about that fellow named Eutychus who listened to Paul preach and fell out of a third-story window (Acts 20:9)? Don't worry, he recovered . . . but are you going to sit there and tell me God didn't find humor in that scenario?

Think of how many times preachers have gotten their tongues twisted and blurted out stupid stuff. Once while I was explaining that many of the people in Christ's day expected Him to come and break the yoke of Rome, out came "roke of Yome." But that wasn't nearly as bad as the time I was describing the unusual strategy Joshua and his warriors employed to bring down the walls of Jericho. Instead of saying they were to march around the wall, I chose to say that they circumscribed the wall, but inadvertently it came out, "circumcised the wall" . . . which brought the house down. You're telling me God didn't laugh?

One of my mentors tells me that he was once introduced by a country preacher as "the professor of the Suppository Preaching Department." I asked him what he did after he got up to preach. He smiled and said, "Well, Chuck, I just stood up and supposited the Word, like I always do." Surely the God we serve finds those moments as funny as we do.

And what about those embarrassing typos and misworded announcements that appear in church bulletins, like:

- This afternoon there will be a meeting in the north and south ends of the church. Children will be baptized at both ends.

- The choir will be participating in the local community sing, which is open to everyone. They will be sinning at 6:00 p.m. this Sunday.

- There will be a sin-in at the Johnsons' home this evening, immediately following the pastor's message, "Intimate Fellowship."

- Affirmation of Faith No. 738: "The Apostles' Greed"

- Solo: "There Is a Bomb in Gilead"

- Order of Service: Silent Prayer and Medication

- This was printed after a church potluck: "Ladies, if you have missing bowels, you will find them in the church kitchen."
- Pastor Brown will marry his son next Sunday morning.

Such stories abound! And you will never convince me that God doesn't get a kick out of such things and laugh with some of us in our well-meant seriousness.

I believe He fully understands us in our imperfect humanity. He understands little children who pick their noses in church because they are bored stiff. It's no big deal to Him. He must smile at some of the notes children send their pastor, too, like this one I read recently:

Dear Pastor,
   I know God loves everybody, but He never met my sister.

Yours sincerely,
Arnold

A friend of mine told me about another one that read:

Dear Paster,
   My father couldn't give more $$money$$ to the chrch. HE is a good chrischen but has a *cheap* boss.

Ronald

Surely God smiles with understanding when he hears prayers like the one Erma Bombeck says she has prayed for years: "Lord, if you can't make me thin, then make my friends look fat."

Isn't God the One who urges us to "Make a joyful noise unto the Lord"? Why do we always think that means singing? Seems to me the most obvious joyful noise on earth is laughter. We say we believe in laughing and having a happy countenance. I'm not sure. I've seen folks quote verses like "Rejoice in the Lord always" while their faces look like they just buried a rich uncle who willed everything to his pregnant guinea pig. Something is missing.

We all *look* so much better and *feel* so much better when we laugh. I don't know of a more contagious sound. And yet there are so many who never weary of telling us, "Life is no laughing matter." It may not be for them, but I must tell you, it often is for me. Knowing that God is causing "all things to work together for good," and remembering that we, His people, are on our way to an eternal home in the heavens without fears or tears, takes the sting out of this temporary parenthesis of time called earthly life.

The returning prodigal was absolutely amazed by his father's immediate acceptance, reckless forgiveness, and unconditional love. Having been so distant, so desperate, so utterly alone, he knew no way to turn but homeward. Then, at the end of his rope, he found himself suddenly safe in his dad's embrace, smothered with kisses, and surrounded by extravagant grace. The fatted calf . . . a soft, warm robe, comfortable new sandals, and the costliest ring were all his . . . no strings attached . . . no probation required. Not surprisingly, that home was soon filled with "music and dancing." As Jesus told the story, He was careful to add, "And they began to be merry."

Then why shouldn't we?

Throughout these pages I have been urging you to lighten up. I could not have done so without knowing that Someone, like the prodigal's father, is diligently searching for you. Every day He scans the horizon and waits patiently for you to appear. He has spared no expense. A blood-smeared cross on which His Son died is now a painful memory, but it was essential to solve the sin problem.

Every day He says to our world, "All is forgiven . . . come on home." His arms are open, and there is a wide, wide smile on His face. The band is tuning up. The banquet is ready to be served. All that is needed is you.

Come on home. You will be so glad you did. In fact, before you know it, you'll begin to laugh again.

Notes

Introduction

1. James S. Huett, ed., *Illustrations Unlimited* (Wheaton, Ill.: Tyndale, 1988), 101.

Chapter 1 / Your Smile Increases Your Face Value

1. G. K. Chesterton, *Orthodoxy* (New York: Dodd, Mead and Co., 1954), 298.

2. Adapted from "The Chair Recognizes Mr. Buckley," quoted in *Tabletalk* 17, no. 1 (March 1992): 9.

3. Jane Canfield, in *Quote/Unquote,* comp. Lloyd Cory (Wheaton, Ill.: Victor Books, 1977), 144.

4. Helen Mallicoat, "I Am," in Tim Hansel, *Holy Sweat* (Waco, Tex.: Word Books, 1987), 136. Used by permission.

5. Hansel, *Holy Sweat,* 58–59.

Chapter 2 / Set Your Sails for Joy

1. Ella Wheeler Wilcox, "The Wind of Fate," in *The Best Loved Poems of the American People,* comp. Hazel Felleman (Garden City, N.Y.: Garden City Books, 1936), 364.

2. Kenneth S. Wuest, *Philippians in the Greek New Testament* (Grand Rapids, Mich.: William B. Eerdmans Publishing Co., 1942), 26–27.

3. William Griffin, "On Making Saints," *Publishers Weekly,* 5 October 1990, 34.

4. Anonymous.

5. John Powell, *Why Am I Afraid to Tell You Who I Am?* (Chicago, Ill.: Argus Communications Co., 1969), 54–55.

6. Ibid., 56.

7. Ibid., 56–57.

8. Ibid., 57–58.

9. Ibid., 61–62.

10. Howard Taylor and Mary G. Taylor, *Hudson Taylor's Spiritual Secret* (Chicago: Moody Press, 1932), 152.

11. Wilcox, "The Wind of Fate," 364.

Chapter 3 / What a Way to Live!

1. G. W. Target, "The Window," from *The Window and Other Essays* (Boise, Idaho: Pacific Press Publishing Association, 1973), 5–7.

2. Stuart Briscoe, *Bound for Joy: Philippians—Paul's Letter from Prison* (Glendale, Calif.: Regal Books, 1975), 25.

3. Samuel Johnson to Lord Chesterfield, 19 September 1777, cited in John Bartlett, *Familiar Quotations,* ed. Emily Morison Beck (Boston, Mass.: Little, Brown and Co., 1980), 355.

4. Anonymous.

Chapter 4 / Laughing Through Life's Dilemmas

1. From "Jesus Is All the World to Me," Will L. Thompson [1847–1909].

2. Horatius Bonar, "Thy Way, Not Mine," *Baker's Pocket Treasury of Religious Verse,* ed. Donald T. Kauffmann (Grand Rapids, Mich.: Baker Book House, 1962), 219. Used by permission.

3. Anonymous.

4. Quoted by J. Foster, *Then and Now* (London, 1945), 83, cited in Ralph P. Martin, *The Epistle of Paul to the Philippians* (Grand Rapids, Mich.: William B. Eerdmans Publishing Co., 1959), 88.

5. "God's Gargoyle: An Interview with Malcolm Muggeridge," *Radix/Right On* (May 1975): 3.

Chapter 5 / The Hidden Secret of a Happy Life

1. Canfield, *Quote/Unquote,* 23.

2. From "When I Survey the Wondrous Cross," Isaac Watts [1674–1748].

3. Harry A. Ironside, *Notes on the Epistle to the Philippians* (Neptune, N.J.: Loizeaux Brothers, 1922), 38–39.

4. D. Martyn Lloyd-Jones, *The Life of Joy: An Exposition of Philippians 1 and 2* (Grand Rapids, Mich.: Baker Book House, 1989), 142–43.

5. Ironside, *Notes on the Epistle to the Philippians*, 47.

6. From "Holy, Holy, Is What the Angels Sing," Rev. Johnson Oatman, Jr.

Chapter 6 / While Laughing, Keep Your Balance!

1. "Advice to a (Bored) Young Man," cited in Ted W. Engstrom, *Motivation to Last a Lifetime* (Grand Rapids, Mich.: Zondervan, 1984), 23–24.

2. Mark Twain, *Pudd'nhead Wilson* [1894], "Pudd'nhead Wilson's Calendar," cited in Bartlett, *Familiar Quotations*, 624.

3. Jimmy Bowen, cited in Sharon Bernstein, "When Entertainment LipSyncs Modern Life," *Los Angeles Times*, 29 November 1990, F1.

4. Ibid.

5. Eugene H. Peterson, *Five Smooth Stones for Pastoral Work* (Atlanta, Ga.: John Knox Press, 1980), 47.

6. J. B. Priestly in *Macmillan Dictionary of Quotations* (Norwalk, Conn.: Easton Press, 1989), 120.

7. "World May End with a Splash," *Los Angeles Times*, 9 October 1982.

8. Julia Seton, *Quote/Unquote*, 67.

9. Laurence Peter and Bill Dana, *The Laughter Prescription* (New York: Ballantine Books, 1987), 8.

10. Jim McGuiggan, *The Irish Papers* (Fort Worth, Tex.: Star Bible Publications, 1992), 42.

11. John Wooden, *They Call Me Coach* (Waco, Tex.: Word Books, 1972), 184.

12. Source unknown.

Chapter 7 / Friends Make Life More Fun

1. Michael LeBoeuf, *How to Win Customers and Keep Them for Life* (New York: Berkley Books, 1987), 84–85.

2. "How Important Are You," © United Technologies Corporation, 1983. Used by permission.

3. Briscoe, *Bound for Joy*, 92–93.

4. Leighton Ford, *Transforming Leadership* (Downers Grove, Ill.: InterVarsity Press, 1991), 139–41.

5. J. B. Lightfoot, *St Paul's Epistle to the Philippians* (London: Macmillan and Co., 1908), 123.

6. William Hendriksen, *New Testament Commentary* (Grand Rapids, Mich.: Baker Book House, 1962), 144–45.

Chapter 8 / Happy Hopes for High Achievers

1. Joe Lomusio, *If I Should Die Before I Live* (Fullerton, Calif.: R. C. Law & Co., 1989), 144–45.

2. Tim Hansel, *When I Relax I Feel Guilty* (Elgin, Ill.: David C. Cook Publishing Co., 1979), 20–22.

3. G. K. Chesterton, *The Napoleon of Notting Hill* (New York: Paulist Press, 1978), 37.

4. William Barclay, *The Mind of St Paul* (New York: Harper and Brothers Publishers, 1958), 17–19.

5. Archibald T. Robertson, *Word Pictures in the New Testament,* vol. 4 (Nashville, Tenn.: Broadman Press, 1931), 453.

6. "I Met My Master," *Poems That Preach,* ed. John R. Rice (Wheaton, Ill.: Sword of the Lord Publishers, 1952), 18. Used by permission.

Chapter 9 / Hanging Tough Together . . . and Loving It

1. *Los Angeles Times,* 27 January 1991.

2. Henry David Thoreau, cited in Bartlett, *Familiar Quotations,* 590.

3. John Pollock, *The Man Who Shook the World* (Wheaton, Ill.: Victor Books, 1972), 18.

4. Robert Ballard, "A Long Last Look at Titanic," *National Geographic* 170, no. 6 (December 1986): 698–705.

5. Bob Benson, *Laughter in the Walls* (Nashville, Tenn.: Impact Books, 1969), 16–17. Used by permission.

6. Benjamin Franklin, at the signing of the Declaration of Independence [4 July 1776], cited in Bartlett, *Familiar Quotations,* 348.

7. From "Higher Ground," Johnson Oatman, Jr. [1856–1926].

Notes

Chapter 10 / It's a Mad, Bad, Sad World, But . . .

1. Flannery O'Connor, *Mystery and Manners* (New York: Farrar, Straus and Giroux, 1969), 167.

2. A. W. Tozer, *The Root of Righteousness* (Harrisburg, Pa.: Christian Publications, 1955), 156.

3. Norman Cousins, *Anatomy of an Illness as Perceived by the Patient* (New York: Norton, 1979), 25–43.

4 G. K. Chesterton, *The Common Man* (New York: Sheed and Ward, 1950), 157–58.

5. Barbara Johnson, *Splashes of Joy in the Cesspools of Life* (Dallas, Tex.: Word Publishing, 1992), 65.

Chapter 11 / Defusing Disharmony

1. Karen Mains, *The Key to a Loving Heart* (Elgin, Ill: David C. Cook, 1979), 143–44.

2. Thomas Brookes, *The Golden Treasure of Puritan Quotations,* ed. I. D. E. Thomas (Chicago, Ill.: Moody Press, 1975), 304.

3. Marshall Shelley, *Well-Intentioned Dragons* (Waco, Tex.: Word Books/CTi, 1985), 11–12.

4. Leslie B. Flynn, *You Don't Have to Go It Alone* (Denver, Colo.: Accent Books, 1981), 117.

Chapter 12 / Freeing Yourself Up to Laugh Again

1. Jean Jacques Rousseau, *Du Contrat Social* [1762], bk. 1, chap. 1, cited in Bartlett, *Familiar Quotations,* 358.

2. W. Grant Lee, in Bartlett, *Familiar Quotations,* 174.

3. Fred Allen, in *Quote/Unquote,* 174.

4. Ruth Harms Calkin, "Spiritual Retreat," *Lord, You Love to Say Yes* (Elgin, Ill.: David C. Cook, 1976), 16–17. Used by permission.

5. Quoted by Ruth Bell Graham, *Prodigals and Those Who Love Them* (Colorado Springs, Colo.: Focus on the Family Publishing, 1991), 44.

Chapter 13 / *Don't Forget to Have Fun As You Grow Up*

1. Anonymous.

2. Fred Cook, in *Quote/Unquote*, 200.

3. Max DePree, *Leadership Is an Art* (New York: Dell Publishing, 1987), 7–10. Used by permission of Doubleday, a division of Bantam Doubleday Dell Publishing Group, Inc.

4. Sophie Tucker, quoted in Rosalind Russell and Chris Chase, *Life Is a Banquet* (New York: Random House, 1977), 2.

5. Quoted in "I Made Mistakes," interview with Richard Dortch, *Christianity Today*, 18 March 1988, 46–47.

6. Ibid.

7. Jeanne Hendricks, *Afternoon* (Nashville, Tenn.: Thomas Nelson Publishers, 1979), 103.

Chapter 14 / *A Joyful, Grace-Filled Good-bye*

1. From the California Newspaper Association.

2. G. Campbell Morgan, *The Unfolding Message of the Bible* (Westwood, N.J.: Fleming H. Revell Co., 1961), 367.

3. J. B. Lightfoot, *Notes on the Epistle to the Philippians*, 171.

4. W. M. Ramsay, *St Paul, the Traveller and the Roman Citizen* (London: Hodder and Stoughton, 1895), 352–53.

5. Alfred Plummer, *A Commentary on St Paul's Epistle to the Philippians* (London: Robert Scott Roxburghe House, 1919), 107.

6. From "Amazing Grace," John Newton [1725–1807].